THE HAPPY, HEALTHY ARTIST

WORRY LESS, IMPROVE YOUR HEALTH & CREATE A SUSTAINABLE CREATIVE CAREER

CASSANDRA GAISFORD

BLUE GIRAFFE PUBLISHING

THE HAPPY, HEALTHY ARTIST

DO LESS & MAKE MORE

CASSANDRA GAISFORD

PRAISE FOR THE HAPPY, HEALTHY ARTIST

"If, like me, you suffer from self-doubt that leads straight to procrastination then this book is for you. Like all of Cassandra's books, this one's a keeper. Healthy writing habits - and mindset habits - are crucial for long-term success. Having Cassandra on our shoulder, pointing the way, makes the journey just that much easier. Thanks for another thought-provoking read, Cassandra. Keep them coming."

~ Melinda Hammond, Writer on the Road

"Gently, and conversationally, *The Happy, Healthy Artist* offers strategies for seeing and thinking differently. For many people the approach is nothing less than transformational."

~ Lawrence Ford

"Loved the fact it is an easy read and is so incredibly comprehensive in its spectrum of tools covered: eastern and western/physical and psychological/science and esoteric. It's hard to find books that capture this in one space–a comprehensive manual containing a tasting platter of techniques."

~ Tina Drummond, Health and Safety Consultant, Wellness Motivator

"Cassandra has mastered the art of speaking in clear and simple terms and has presented *Bounce* as an easy to read, concise—yet completely comprehensive guide to overcoming all the obstacles that stand between yourself and your passion. She has taken a truly holistic approach and leaves no stone unturned. She lays out all the facets of overcoming your obstacles in a no-nonsense fashion and covers everything ... Mind, body and soul ... the physical, the spiritual, and the scientific. She evens touches on topics that may be considered 'airy-fairy' with believable and inspiring confidence. Do not be fooled by its quick two-hour read, it is incredibly comprehensive astoundingly holistic—and effective.

~ Niki Firth, Amazon Review

DEDICATION

This book is dedicated to joy

HAPPY AT WORK

"In order that people may be happy in their work, these things are needed: They must be fit for it: They must not do too much of it; And they must have a sense of success in it."

~ John Ruskin, Victorian social reformer and artist

AUTHOR'S NOTE

I love being an artist. Creativity is my passion—my joy. And I'm good at it. I'm an award-winning artist, a prolific author and the Amazon #1 bestselling author of over twenty non-fiction books, including, *How to Find Your Passion and Purpose, Mid-Life Career Rescue, Bounce, The Prosperous Author: Millionaire Mindset*, and *The Art of Success*.

As Mollie Mathews, I also have fun writing romance novels, including *Flight of Passion, Love in Venice, The Italian Billionaire's Christmas Bride,* and *Married by Christmas*.

Because I love what I do my vocation doesn't feel like work at all. In fact, just the opposite. But if I'm not careful I forget to look out for me. I forget to eat. I forget to stretch my legs, I forget to program my mindset for success—and all the other health behaviors that sustain my writing and creative career.

Stress, burnout, anxiety, and depression descend and before long I doubt I am an artist. I doubt I can write, paint, take beautiful photos or do anything creative. I stop believing I can make a living from my writing and my creativity. I lose my joy.

If you've been drawn to this book you may feel like this too. Perhaps you're already feeling burned out, anxious, or stressed too. Like one of my author friends who recently wrote on a forum, *"Defi-*

nitely feeling the solopreneur/authorpreneur roller coaster lately. I'm at a low point and wondering if I'm heading backwards. For those of you who are full time "preneurs", how do you cope with uncertainty, fluctuating income, anxiety?"

Or Paul, who shared that since quitting his salaried position he's never worked harder in his life. For Paul, and others like him, working 18-hour days has become the new norm.

Working horrendous hours is not sustainable if you want a long-term career. But there is a way to work smarter, not harder, do less and achieve more, maintain your health and sanity, and elevate your prosperous productivity—and you'll find the elixir that turns stress back into joy in *The Happy, Healthy Artist*.

As a bestselling author, award-winning artist, holistic psychologist, and creativity expert (BCA, Dip Psych) in *The Happy, Healthy Artist* I challenge the myth of the overworked, burned out artist.

In this book I share dozens of insights based on survey research, my professional achievements and the success secrets of extraordinary artists, authors and creative entrepreneurs like Tim Ferriss, Coco Chanel, Leonardo da Vinci, James Patterson, Paulo Coelho, Nora Roberts, Arianna Huffington, Oprah, Isabel Allende, Zaha Hadid, Georgia O'Keeffe, and many more.

These successful authors and artists know the ultimate success secret—*your health is your wealth* and the gateway to prosperous productivity.

In *The Happy, Healthy Artist*, I'll share with you the things I've learned figuring out how to make a living from my creativity.

As you'll discover, being prosperous and productive is not just about money; it's also about health, happiness, close relationships, living a meaningful life, and enjoying life's journey.

A simple tweak, here and there, or kicking an energy-zapping habit may be just the boost you need.

As one reader wrote to me: "I'm emailing you to let you know the impact your book has had on me. I cold-turkey stopped imbibing alcohol and coke and I've gained twenty years in energy. We all know we don't drink a lot but what an insidious thing nightly alcohol is…Thank you for your book - it's become a bit of a bible, or should I say they've become bits of bibles."

I'm so pleased to know this! It's amazing how much productivity is gained by making changes to our health habits.

My hope is that next time you are feeling discouraged, overwhelmed, or faced with adversity, two simple words will come to mind: 'Health and Joy.' And then, having been reminded that loving what you do, and valuing your well-being will empower your long-term career, that you will then go quickly into health mode and apply the strategies you have learned in this book.

If when next faced with a challenge, your default thoughts are 'healthy joy', and 'how can I spark joy and empower my health?' then I will consider this book a success.

ABOUT THIS BOOK

This book offers short, sound-bites of stand-alone readings designed to help you cultivate resilience and awareness amid the challenges of earning a daily living.

More than a collection of thoughts for the day, *The Happy Healthy Artist* offers a progressive program of holistic—mental, emotional, physical and spiritual—study, guiding you through essential concepts, themes, and practices on the path to prosperous productivity, well-being, joy, and happiness.

The teachings are gently humorous, sometimes challenging, occasionally provocative, but always compassionate and kind, and, I hope, seemingly infinitely wise.

All that I share are strategies that have worked for me personally through many of my own creative challenges, and for my clients in my professional work as a holistic psychologist and creativity coach.

The Happy, Healthy Artist features the most essential and stirring passages from my previous books, exploring topics such as: meditation, mindfulness, positive health behaviors, and working with fear, depression, anxiety, and other painful emotions.

The Happy, Healthy Artist expands upon my previous books in that it encourages a more playful and mindful approach to the seriousness of life and the ever-present stressors we all face.

Through the course of this book, you will learn practical, creative and simple methods for heightening awareness and overcoming habitual patterns that block happiness and joy and hold you back.

Brimming with a smorgasbord of easy to apply strategies that will boost your mental, emotional and physical well-being, *The Happy, Healthy Artist* is a timeless call to action for anyone who wants to create a sustainable, joyful, writing and creative career.

- If you want to write and create with passion, purpose, and joy
- If you want to have more energy and fire in your belly
- If you want to overcome procrastination, or creative inertia
- If you want to preserve your relationships
- If you want to do less and earn more
- If you want to create a long-term writing or artistic career…

Then *The Happy, Healthy Artist* is exactly the right the book for you —whoever you are, whatever you ache to create, and however you define health, happiness, and prosperity.

The ideas described in this book apply to anyone who's trying to inject some purposeful creative productivity into their life and work.

Your Caffeine Hit

Think of *The Happy, Healthy Artist* like a shot of espresso. Sometimes one quick hit is all it takes to get started. But sometimes you need a few shots to sustain your energy. Or maybe you need a bigger motivational hit and then you're on your way.

You're in control of what works best for you. Go at your own pace, but resist over-caffeinating. A little bit of guidance here and there can do as much to fast-track your success as consuming all the principles in one hit.

The beginning of this book focuses on strategies to increase your awareness of what makes you happy. When you're stressed this knowledge can be one of the first things to go.

You'll discover ways to increase happiness, reduce stress, minimize anxiety and reclaim joy in Part Two and the chapters that follow.

Part three will identify common obstacles to success, help you slay a path through them, and empower your tenacity to persevere with your creative calling.

Skim to sections that are most relevant to you, and return to familiar ground to reinforce home-truths. But most of all, enjoy your experience.

Stress Less, Love More & Create a Sustainable Writing or Artistic Career Today!

Let's get moving…

WHAT MAKES YOU HAPPY? ASPIRE TO MAKE A DIFFERENCE

"Remember that just because you're doing a lot more doesn't mean you're getting a lot more done. Don't confuse movement with progress. My mother told me, she said, 'Yeah, because you can run in one place all the time and never get anywhere.'

"Continue to strive, continue to have goals, continue to progress and anything you want—good, you can have it. Claim it, work hard to get it, when you get it, reach back, pull someone else up. Each one, teach one.

"Don't just aspire to make a living. Aspire to make a difference."

~ Denzel Washington, actor

1

PURPOSEFUL PRODUCTIVITY

Create an extraordinary life by prioritizing your purpose. By living your soul purpose, and sharing your gifts with the world, you consciously or unconsciously tap into universal needs and higher levels of consciousness. This boosts your energy, elevates your success, and yields mind-bending productivity. All of which enables phenomenal results.

Paulo Coelho, for example, wrote *The Alchemist* in less than two weeks following his own search for meaning and purpose. The book's main theme is about finding one's destiny. And it's a theme that tapped a universal chord.

Your purpose communicates who you are, clarifies your priorities, and determines the creations your actions produce.

BENEFITS OF CREATING with purpose include:

- Tapping into your life's purpose gives you an edge; it stokes the flames of passion, enthusiasm, drive, and tenacity needed to succeed

- A sense of purpose can give you the courage, and clarity of vision needed to thrive
- Purpose fuels the embers of flagging motivation and latent dreams
- A sense of purpose can lead you to the work you were born to do and enable you to be free to be authentically and purposefully you
- Discovering your true calling opens you up to the dreams the Universe has for you—bigger than you may dream for yourself
- Creating with purpose connects you with divine intelligence, universal energy, and the laws of attraction—magnetizing fans to you

A LIFE LIVED on purpose is the most meaningful, powerful and happiest.

IF YOU NEED MORE HELP to find and live your life purpose you can read my book, *Find Your Passion and Purpose: Four Easy Steps to Discover a Job You Want and Live the Life You Love*, available as an audiobook paperback, hardback and eBook from all good online book retailers.

Or you may prefer to take my online course, and watch inspirational and practical videos and other strategies to help you to fulfil your potential—https://the-coaching-lab.teachable.com/p/follow-your-passion-and-purpose-to-prosperity.

2

FOLLOW YOUR PASSION

Passion is a source of unlimited energy from your soul that enables you to achieve extraordinary results. It's the fire that ignites your potential and inspires you to be who you really are.

Following your passion and claiming your authentic self is a great way to boost your vitality. Whether you call it joy, love or obsession or desire, these powerful heart-felt emotions are natural opiates for your mind, body, and soul.

Sadly, when you're feeling anxious, depressed or stressed, the things that you love are the first things to be traded. Nothing seems to spark joy. But, when you do something that feeds your soul you may be amazed at how quickly fire ignites.

Passion brings the energy or chi of love, giving you energy, vitality and a heightened sense of well-being. It's one of the greatest stress-busters of all and promotes the generation of endorphins—feel-good chemicals that will give you an extra spring in your step.

THE POWER OF PASSION

"Nothing great in the world has been accomplished without passion," the philosopher G.W.F. Hegel once said. Denzel Washington and many other successful creative people agree. "You only live once, so do what you feel passionate about, take chances professionally, don't be afraid to fail," Washington says.

- Passion is energy. Without energy, you have nothing.
- To be passionate is to be fully alive.
- Passion is about emotion, feeling, zest, and enthusiasm.
- Passion is about intensity, fervor, ardor, and zeal.
- Passion is about fire.
- Passion is about eagerness and preoccupation.
- Passion is about excitement and animation.
- Passion is about determination and self-belief.
- Passion, like love and joy, is contagious.
- Passion can't be faked. It's the mark of authenticity.

"What you write becomes who you are . . . So make sure you love what you write!" says J.K. Rowling.

Passion fuels inner purpose and fires the flames of your imagination. It gives you a reason for living and the confidence and drive to pursue your dreams. Passion enables you to unleash latent forces and God-given talents.

When you follow your passion, you'll find your sweet spot. You'll be emboldened by love— thus powering your creativity, courage, resolve, and tenacity. You'll also bounce back from setbacks, and refuse to allow failure to stop you—increasing your likelihood of achieving extraordinary success.

Focus on what excites you. "I find things I like and I do them," says James Patterson, arguably one of the most financially successful authors today.

Feel the power that comes from focusing on what excites you. What do you love doing? What inspires you? What makes you feel joyful?

Channel your passions into your creative career. Even five minutes a day doing something you love can give you back your mojo.

3

JUMPING WITH JOY

Joy has phenomenal energy and incredible versatility. In *The Book of Joy* the Dalai Lama shares that Paul Ekman, longtime friend and famed emotions researcher, has written that joy is associated with feelings as varied as:

- Pleasure (of the five senses)
- Amusement (from a chuckle to a belly laugh)
- Contentment (a calmer kind of satisfaction)
- Excitement (in response to novelty or challenge)
- Relief (following upon another emotion, such as fear, anxiety, and even pleasure)
- Wonder (before something astonishing and admirable)
- Ecstasy or bliss (transporting us outside ourselves)
- Exultation (at having accomplished a difficult or daring task)
- Radiant pride (when our children earn a special honor)
- Elevation (from having witnessed an act of kindness, generosity, or compassion)
- Gratitude (the appreciation of a selfless act of which one is the beneficiary)

Buddhist scholar and former scientist Matthieu Ricard has added three other more exalted states of joy: rejoicing (in someone else's happiness, what Buddhists call mudita) delight or enchantment (a shining kind of contentment) spiritual radiance (a serene joy born from deep well-being and benevolence).

When you tap into your joy, you tap into an unlimited reservoir of energy and enthusiasm.

The French take it further—of course! *Jouissance*, literally means orgasmic joy. It's derived from the word from *jouir* ("to enjoy"). *Jouissance* is to enjoy something a lot!

One of my favorite creativity experts Mihaly Czikszentmihaly, refers to this as a state of "flow."

In a popular YouTube talk he asks, "What makes a life worth living? Money cannot make us happy," he says. Instead, he urges us to learn from people who find pleasure and lasting satisfaction in activities that bring about this state of transcendent flow.

Coco Chanel was flowing when she designed her clothes, she was flowing when she attended to the minutest details of her garments. For her, her work had a spiritual aspect, it wasn't a job, it was her vocation and her deepest purpose—to liberate women from corsets and clothes that constricted their freedom.

"Ask someone born under the sign of Leo about the secret of leadership or a successful life and they will invariably list passion and tenacity, and a predisposition towards joy as the proper tools for the job," writes Steven Weiss in his book, *Signs of Success: The Remarkable Power of Business Astrology*.

As a Leo, Coco Chanel exemplified this. She knew that you can succeed at almost anything if you follow your joy. This is where you soul meets the road—accelerating you toward your preferred future and fueling your success.

Find something that sparks joy and keep hugely interested in it by feeding and nurturing your *jouissance* every day.

Encourage yourself, challenge any mistaken assumptions and boost your belief by collecting examples of people who followed their joy and made a rewarding career or enriched their lives.

Need help to find your joy and purpose? You'll find plenty of help in my book, *How to Find Your Joy and Purpose: Four Easy Steps to Discover A Job You Want And Live the Life You Love.*

4

EFFORTLESS BLISS

Some of the most common questions I'm asked by people who seeking coaching is, "How can I find out what I'm good at? What are my talents?" and "How can I be sure that I will enjoy it and succeed?"

Whilst the answers may be evasive, the past is often a good predictor of the future. Often you just need reminding of the times and circumstances in your life when you felt inspired or energized by something, when your skills just seemed to flow, and of the outcomes, successes and positive feedback you achieved. These moments of bounce provide important clues to your passions and unique strengths and talents.

Effortless bliss happens without force. It's the sheer state of joy and transcendence you experience when you're in that state of flow which I referred to in the previous chapter.

When you follow your bliss, some people believe this is where our capacity for genius resides. "The Greeks believed our genius was not part of us but was a divine visitation.

"Our jobs, as artists and writers, was to become the best possible vessel for that genius. Part of that is to be forever learning, improving, expanding, and experimenting," writes Jessa Crispin in her fabulous book, *The Creative Tarot: A Modern Guide to an Inspired Life*.

Bliss is the home of our God-given talents, and to activate their potential and reap the benefits we need to bring them out to play.

"The accompanying state of joy is quite distinct from the thrill of success; it is a joy of inner peace and oneness with all of life," writes David Hawkins in his fabulous book, *Power vs. Force: The Hidden Determinants of Human Behavior*.

To reach this state of bliss often requires a willingness to step outside your current comfort zone and challenge yourself to soar beyond what you know.

"It is notable that this transcendence of the personal self and surrender to the very essence or spirit of life often occur at a point just beyond the apparent limit of the athlete's ability," says Hawkins.

I experienced this when I embarked on my first attempt at writing an historical novel. Some of the early feedback I received included, "Sheer brilliance." No one was more surprised than me.

The words and ideas just seemed to flow.

"This phenomenon," says Hawkins, "Is commonly described in terms of pushing oneself to the point where one suddenly breaks through a performance barrier and the activity then miraculously becomes effortless; the body then seems to move with grace and ease of its own accord, as though animated by some invisible force."

I also lose all track of time when I am painting. The most fulfilling part of this is creating something that is innately satisfying to me and that the recipient truly loves. I feel excited, energized, and truly complete.

I feel a huge sense of purpose and people comment positively about my flow-inspired works and tell me how something I created changed their life.

Writing books, posts and articles that help people to follow their bliss comes easily to me and produces the same state.

I won an art award once, and my first attempt at an oil painting was selected as a finalist in a prestigious portraiture award. It seemed so effortless that I was completely thrown.

I don't say this to boast, but I wanted to share with you that in both cases, and many more, I always experienced self-doubt, and I never possessed the confidence or believed I had talent, but I did what made my soul sing, and challenged myself to show up and share my work anyway.

Perhaps you may set yourself a similar 'stretch' goal, or you may be blissfully content to explore what energizes you and keep your talents hidden. Either way, it is in the act of following your bliss that you will find great joy and personal fulfillment.

5

FINISH WHAT YOU START

Nothing improves your mindset more than a sense of achievement. The opposite is also true—leaving projects unfinished fuels feelings of failure.

Whatever I'm doing I get very guilty if I don't put a good day's work in. I'm not one for making excuses. I had this Catholic upbringing. I was taught to finish what you start," Nora Roberts once said.

Leaving tasks hanging increases anxiety, depression, and feelings of unworthiness. Don't do this to yourself. I know how destructive this can be to your confidence—and success. For years I had half-written manuscripts clogging up my mind and computer.

People around me began to get frustrated, annoyed, and cross. My cheerleaders began to give up on me. I almost gave up on myself. Finally, in my fifties, I channeled this horrendous frustration into finishing my books. One of my helpful enabling mantras was, "Done is better than perfect."

I published three non-fiction books in four months—all of them shot to #1 on Amazon. You can do this! In Book Two of the *Prosperity for Authors* series, you'll learn powerhouse productivity tools you can harness to help you finish what you start.

What's important now is devotion. Devote yourself to the energy of your creative project. Devote yourself to the inspiration that planted the fire in your belly. Devote yourself to completing your art.

A devoted person is a loyal person.

As playwright and novelist Henry Miller once said, "Start no more new books, add no more new material to existing books. Work on one thing at a time until finished."

Your reward for finishing will be the satisfaction of seeing your baby fly into the world, and the joy of having space to give birth to new works of heart.

How can you become devoted to finishing your books and increase your ability to complete your projects? What do you need to do more or less of, start doing, or stop doing?

Learn how to "knock the bugger off" in the section, Overcoming Obstacles later in this book! I share a super inspiring story to encourage you to persevere with your dreams.

6

BECOME AUDACIOUSLY OBSESSED

Nothing boosts productivity and joy more than a healthy obsession. A healthy obsession can be a liberating and clarifying catalyst to your true calling and career direction—especially for people in the mid-life zone. With maturity comes renewed confidence and determination to pursue, and write about, the things they are truly passionate about.

Passion, some say, can be difficult to find, but if you're awake it will find you. Stay open-hearted and open-minded. Don't be like so many adults who fail to discover it all together, and in the absence of any encouragement, give up.

"People pride themselves upon their willpower, their indomitable courage, upon the fact that nothing frightens them," writes T. Lobsang Rampa, in his classic book *You Forever*.

"They assured bored listeners that with their willpower they can do anything at all." But the truth is there is no greater power than imagination, passion, and the incredible power of love.

"The Last Supper soon became my obsession," writes Spanish author Javier Sierra in his book *The Secret Supper*, a dazzling historical thriller.

His novels all have a "secret" common purpose: to solve historical musketries based on real documentation and extensive field research.

Javier's passion and his obsession have made him a bestseller author throughout the world.

Similarly, Joe Medeiros, a writer, and producer, known for The Tonight Show with Jay Leno, developed an obsession for Leonardo da Vinci's iconic portrait of the Mona Lisa after reading about its theft from the Louvre.

Medeiros' obsession had a singular focus—discovering the truth. He first learned that the Mona Lisa was stolen when he was 25 and spent the next 30 years trying to discover the thief's motivation—a simple Italian immigrant named Vincenzo Peruggia who worked as a house painter in Paris.

When asked why he was so fascinated by the story, and why he devoted over 35 years to his quest, Medeiros said, "The fact that that I couldn't solve the mystery. I wasn't able to write it as a [fictional] screenplay] but once we started to make the documentary, everything started to fall into place. And I always wanted to know, was he crazy? Did he do it for patriotism, did he do it for money, did someone commission him? I had all these questions and that's what kept me at it until I found the answers."

Because of my own obsession with The Mona Lisa, and also with discovering the truth, I came across Medeiros' wonderful documentary and have since reached out to him to help me with my research for my novel of historical art-related fiction set in Renaissance and modern-day Florence.

Learn more about Medeiros's 35 year obsession here: http://www.monalisamissing.com/single-post/2015/07/19/The-Story-of-the-Film-A-35YearLong-Obsession

Passionate Obsessions Empower Your Productivity, Joy, and Prosperity

A healthy obsession can lead you to many things, including:

- A state of divine flow—enabling you to write with mind-blowing productivity

- Your point of excellence—unleashing dormant talents and natural gifts
- Rocket-fuel tenacity to persevere and succeed
- Mentors, helpful allies and similarly obsessed people who will cheerlead and elevate your success
- A legion of devoted fans who are drawn to your impassioned writing
- Your passion and life purpose—spreading seeds of joy and inspiration and benefiting others
- Your life niche—creating a breath of fresh air and giving you a competitive edge
- True bliss—leading you to your vocation where being paid is the icing on the cake

NEW ZEALAND MOTORCYCLING legend Burt Munro proved that passionate obsession is the key to success. "All my life I've wanted to do something big," he said. In 1967 Burt achieved something huge.

At the age of 68, against all the odds, he set a world record of 183.586 mph with his highly modified Indian Scout motorcycle. To qualify he made a one-way run of 190.07 mph, the fastest ever officially recorded speed on an Indian.

Like for so many inspiring people, the road to success was not an easy one—it involved much personal hardship and numerous setbacks, but armed with his passion and a compelling desire to "go out with a bang," Burt Munro mortgaged his house and set out on the greatest adventure of his life.

His truly awesome achievements were brought to life in an inspiring and uplifting film, *The World's Fastest Indian*.

The World's Fastest Indian not only gives movie-goers an inside look at Munro's passion, but it also gives them an idea of New Zealand filmmaker Roger Donaldson's overwhelming desire to tell the story.

"This project has been a passion of mine since I completed a documentary about Burt Munro back in 1972," Donaldson said. "I have been intrigued by Burt's story for many, many years; some would say my obsession with this film matches Burt's obsession with his bike."

Donaldson's passion for his subject has won him international acclaim from Academy Award-winning actor Anthony Hopkins. "I thought it was a terrific movie. It is a unique script...it is just so well written, very well written, beautifully written, and so refreshing. I've worked with a lot of great directors, Steven Spielberg and Oliver Stone, and Roger Donaldson is there with that lot, you know. He really is," Hopkins said.

What Do You Collect?

Passionate obsessions, as you have begun to discover, go in all directions, and many times they are revealed in your collections. These could be as tangible as exotic butterflies, books, spoons, antiques, paintings, or as intangible as a dream or an idea.

I collect positivity and articles and stories related to people's extraordinary passions. My collections have inspired many of my self-empowerment books.

As I mentioned, I also have a passionate obsession with all things related to Leonardo da Vinci, but particularly his portrait of The Mona Lisa, and I have a burning desire to reveal the truth behind the mysterious life of the woman in the painting, Lisa del Giocondo. I am sure I own every single book every written about both Lisa and Leonardo. My partner once laughed, "There are three of us in this relationship—you, me and The Mona Lisa."

It's true, I am obsessed and enthralled with my research for my historical novel Mona Lisa's Secret and with telling her story. Follow my obsession and sign up to my newsletter and be the first to know when this story will be published—http://eepurl.com/bEArfT. Sign up now and receive a welcome gift—your free "Find your Passion" E-book.

Become audaciously obsessed. Real obsession is more than a fad or a fleeting enthusiasm. It can't be turned on and off like a tap. Answering the following questions will help you begin to clarify the things you have a burning obsession for:

What do you value? What do you need to experience, feel, or be doing to feel deeply fulfilled?

What do you collect? List all your obsessions and the things that interest you deeply. How can your passions fuel obsessive productivity?

Dive Deeper...

If you're struggling to identify your obsessions, you'll find some handy prompts and true stories in my book Find Your Passion and Purpose: Four Easy Steps to Discover a Job You Want and Live the Life You Love. You'll also find inspiration, including true transformational change stories by people like you in my Mid-Life Career Rescue series.

7

SLOW BOUNCE

While we're on the subject of effortlessness, it seems important to talk about peaceful patience. So many people equate speed with progress. Yet, there's something refined and graceful and enduring about things that take their time to flower.

Savor your journey, enjoy the ride, be kind to yourself and be patient during setbacks. Rejoice in steady progress, no matter how small. Slowly chip away at the things most important to you. Learn and grow from any challenges, but don't let them stop you.

Crawl, creep, dally, dawdle or go a the pace of a snail—whatever your tempo, incremental movements forward still equal progress.

Revel in the slow bounce by looking back and appreciating what you have already achieved and how many lives you have positively impacted along the way. Keep your focus away from any lapses you may think you've made. Berating yourself or piling on the guilt won't speed your progress.

Forgive yourself for what you think you've done or haven't done or how little progress you feel you've made. Take heart from Leonardo da Vinci and other enduring icons of success. It's not how quickly you get there, it's the enduring legacy you leave behind that matters most.

8

MIND POWER

Your mind is so incredibly vital to the success or failure of virtually everything you do, from relationships, health, work, and finances to overall happiness.

Thoughts do become things, and your body experiences what the mind believes. This is why challenging and conquering your fears and mistaken beliefs is so important.

Happily, you can trick you mind into gravitating towards what you want and away from what you don't.

"I have learned how to deceive people into health for their benefit. Doctors can kill or cure with 'wordswordswords' when they become 'swordswordswords.' We all have the potential for self-induced healing built into us. The key is to know how to achieve your potential," says Bernie Siegel, M.D., author of *A Book of Miracles* and *The Art of Healing*.

Many of the things that influence your thoughts, feelings, and behaviors are invisible; a great many lurk in the realm of the subconscious mind.

The function of your subconscious mind is to store and retrieve data. Its job is to ensure that you respond exactly the way you are programmed.

"By the time you reach the age of 21, you've already permanently stored more than one hundred times the contents of the entire Encyclopedia Britannica," says motivational writer Brian Tracey.

And much of this information is rubbish, false, incomplete, or obsolete.

Your subconscious mind is like a huge memory bank. Its capacity is virtually unlimited. It permanently stores everything that ever happens to you. What is limited is your ability to consciously recall many of the scripts programmed into your mind.

You may not even be aware of limiting beliefs that are holding you back. Boosting your self-awareness will change that, coupled with a willingness to grow.

One of the most important things you can commit to realizing is that you exist in more than the physical world. The mental world, the emotional world, and the spiritual world all exert a powerful influence over you—whether you are consciously tapping into them or not.

"What most people never realize is that the physical realm is merely a 'printout' of the other three," writes T. Harv Eker.

Any limiting and unhelpful beliefs or repressed experiences preventing you from becoming a prosperous author cannot be changed in the physical world. They can only be changed in the "program"—the mental, emotional, and spiritual worlds.

Which is why *The Happy, Healthy Artist* takes a holistic approach to health and happiness. Passion, joy, faith, prayer, meditation, courage, dreams, purpose, and mindfulness practices are some of the strategies we'll discuss in this book.

YOUR MILLIONAIRE MINDSET

Prosperous productivity isn't everything, but it's often a sign of passion, purpose, capability and drive in those who have acquired it. By thinking like a prosperous millionaire you'll bounce back from setbacks and maximize your likelihood of success.

Your goal may not be to make millions—your goal may be to enjoy following your passion for telling stories, creating inspiring art, expressing yourself and to have fun doing it.

You may wish to earn a small living from your creativity—or a grand one. Whatever your intentions prepare your mindset.

Creating a beautiful mind is one of the most important and effective places you can empower.

9

CULTIVATE A BOUNCE MINDSET

His Holiness the 14th Dalai Lama once said, "Negative thoughts are like weeds, but positive thoughts are like flowers—they need nurturing every day."

Leonardo da Vinci proactively fertilized his mind and empowered his resolve by focusing on his dreams, goals, and aspirations.

"You cannot help being good, because your hand and your mind, being accustomed to gather flowers would ill know how to pluck thorns," he once wrote.

To steady himself against self-doubt or the attacks of others, he actively cultivated a bounce mindset by using affirmations, journaling, meditating, channeling and accessing the spiritual realms, and surrounding himself with like-minded, aspirational and inspirational people. By doing so, he developed grit and the ability to bounce back from extreme adversity.

If you actively cultivate a success mindset you automatically increase your ability to bounce because your mind will create a barrier to discouragement. This helps bounce back the thorns of self-doubt, procrastination, fear, and any of the other things toxic to your happiness and success.

Oprah once said that one of the best ways to cultivate a success mindset is to think like a queen: "A queen is not afraid to fail. Failure is another stepping stone to greatness."

Similarly, J.K. Rowling encourages making failure part of your bounce strategy. "Failure is inevitable—make it a strength," she says. We'll dive deeper into how to fear less and bounce back from failure later in this book.

For now, impress this upon your mind—attitude is everything. As Buddhists say, life is suffering—it's how you react to life that counts. "With our thoughts, we make the world," Buddha once said.

Think royal—cultivate a success mindset and bounce through life like a king or queen.

10

PROSPEROUS PRODUCTIVITY

Are you busy being busy, ticking everything on your endless to-do list, or are you being prosperously productive?

Prosperously productive people:

- Work with purpose
- Set and write goals
- Think big, plan small and get the job done
- Focus—they narrow their concentration to one thing and get the job done
- Believe that time is money, they invest time in things that enable them to work less but earn more
- Play to win, not to avoid defeat
- Visualize what they want—and go for it
- Guard and block-out time—all else is a distraction
- Create "miracles" via their rituals, routines and winning habits
- Focus on growth; they know comfort stunts progress
  Automate and systematize everything they can
- Know that success attracts success; they learn from and

surround themselves with only the best, and network collaboratively with those who can lift them higher
- Never stop learning; they learn from their mistakes pursue greatness and invest in continual improvement
- Control their emotions and maintain a positive mindset Know when to stop working, and balance hard work with personal time for relaxation

For increasing numbers of people, good fortune or being prosperous includes: living authentically; maintaining good health; and having fulfilling relationships, creative freedom, a sense of well-being, peace of mind, happiness and joy.

Prosperity, for some people, means achieving financial freedom. Prosperity also includes the ability to achieve your desires, whatever these may be, and being true to the vision you have for yourself and your life.

Coco Chanel once said, "There are people who have money and people who are rich. How many cares one loses when one decides not to be something, but to be *someone*.

When you commit to being the creator of your life and defining prosperity on your own terms, you choose to enrich your life and you become *"someone."* If earning a living from your writing is your goal, you choose to become a successful author.

If working smarter, not harder and doing less but earning more is your goal, and I'm guessing it is because you've been drawn to this book, you're committed to finding ways that balance effort with ease. Read on to clarify what being productive really means and what it really takes.

11

PURPOSEFUL PRIORITIES

We all want to be more successfully productive but do we really know what this means? What does productivity look like? What does it feel like? How can productivity benefit your life—will it accelerate your wealth, happiness, and fulfillment? What might it steal—your sanity, relationships, health, and wealth?

These are questions many of us never ask—until it's too late. Avoid barking up the wrong tree and chasing an ideal that may lead you further from the things that really matter. Pause for a minute and ask yourself what does being productive mean to you?

"Productivity is the outcome of your efforts," says Laurie Wills, a former bank executive. "It's how much you get out, versus how much you put in. The question you need to ask," he says, "Is when you look at what you're getting out is it what's important to you?"

Dictionary.com defines productivity as, "the quality, state, or fact of being able to generate, create, enhance, or bring forth goods and services."

As a prosperous author making a living from writing, productivity to me means being able to produce quality books that enhance people's lives, solve problems, inspire and enlighten and which people want to buy.

Because I'm a lifestyle authorpreneur who values my life and relationships and my ability to live life as I please, is it means working smarter not harder and doing things that create more wealth and fulfillment the easy way.

Prosperous productivity isn't about being a work slave, being busy staying busy or blazing the midnight oil…It's more about priorities, planning, and fiercely guarding your time.

As Neil Patel, recognized as a top 100 entrepreneur under the age of 30 by President Obama and one of the top 100 entrepreneurs under the age of 35 by the United Nations, once said, "Who cares about being popular if it doesn't make you a single dollar?"

The outcome I really wanted, to make a living from my writing and have fun doing it, was hindered by a seemingly small matter of detail I was never encouraged to give attention to—how to invest my time wisely to make serious money.

Prime your mind for purposeful productivity—what are the outcomes that matter most to you? Money, fulfillment, helping others, worldwide acclaim and adoring fans—or something else?

12

A VISION OF VICTORY

"Begin with the end in mind," encourages Steven Covey in his runaway bestselling book *The Seven Habits of Highly Successful People*.

Your vision is your "why;" it's the furnace that stokes your desire and fuels your dreams. It's the big picture view of your long-term future and aspirations.

If you lack a 'big picture' view, we can easily fall into bad habits, lose your focus, or prematurely give up on a promising career.

What is your vision? What does your prosperous life look like? Is prosperity a passive income that funds your lifestyle? Is it the ability to live and work anywhere in the world? Or is it truckloads of sales and buckets of savings in the bank? Is it one best-selling book and that's it?

Strengthen your vision by clarifying your reasons for wanting to succeed.

"I started to write romance because I needed to make money," says Mary Bly, a tenured professor of English Literature at Fordham University. Bly writes best-selling Regency and Georgian romance novels under her pen name Eloisa James.

When she first started writing romances, she was struggling to pay back the debt incurred during her professional studies—and was soon hooked.

J.K. Rowling was a single mom struggling on a benefit when she began to write the Harry Potter series. I repeat, *series*. Her vision was always long-term success.

"You go where your vision is. Think big, feel big, and know in your heart that you are one with God," says Joseph Murphy, Ph.D., author and New Thought minister.

"And you will project a radiance, a glow, a confidence, a joy, and a healing vibration which blesses all who come within your orbit now and forevermore."

That's the Law of Attraction, the Law of Manifestation, The Law of Intention all wrapped into one.

Define your vision. See it clearly in your mind and heart. Engage all the senses until it becomes your living reality.

13

IMAGINE BETTER

Visualization is one of the most powerful mind exercises you can do. No doubt you've heard the saying, "Out of sight, out of mind." But what, if anything, are you doing to keep your dream of making a living from your creativity visible?

"What practical strategies are you going to implement as a result of reading this book?" I wrote to an advance reader.

Her reply was, "Drawing/painting and writing all the things I have in my mind about my project. Getting my specific passion journal that is solely for my new project out and having it constantly with me, feeding it every day."

Empower your intentions by writing them down, creating a vision board and reviewing your intentions daily. Consider creating a Passion Journal to boost your bounce and manifest your intentions. In the last chapter of this book I share tips and links to help you create a passion journal. Your free gift at the beginning of this book also has helpful strategies.

Another variation of this is to create a prosperity dream board. This is where manifesting your preferred future really happens.

I have covered the wall of my writing room with images of the books I have written and plan to write, feedback from people who have encouraged me on my writer's journey, and feeling-based images of what prosperity means to me—including a photo of me and my partner on vacation (feeling awesome, happy, and free).

Every time I sit in my writing chair looking at my prosperity board, it is a motivational kick-start; a feeling-based affirmation of not only what I yearn for, but the successes I have already manifested.

So many things I've visualized and affirmed on my prosperity board are now my living realities. And the others? I have no doubt that they soon will be!

Creating a sacred space that displays what you want brings it to life. What you focus on expands. Place success, health and happiness center stage. Create visual affirmations and place them in a space where you see them often.

"The law of attraction is forming your entire life experience and it is doing that through your thoughts. When you are visualizing, you are emitting a powerful frequency out into the Universe," writes Rhonda Byrne in her popular book *The Secret*.

Whether you believe in magic or not, we know that visualization works. Olympic athletes have been using it for decades to improve performance. *Psychology Today* reported that the brain patterns activated when a weightlifter lifts heavy weights are also similarly activated when the lifter just imagined (visualized) lifting weights."

Brain Gym

In the traditions of Napoleon Hill, Earl Nightingale and Maxwell Maltz, author Jack Canfield also emphasizes the importance of focusing on a vision and creating compelling and vivid pictures in your mind in order to achieve your goals. Canfield cites neuropsychologists who study expectancy theory to support his view on the significance of visualization.

Scientists once believed that people responded to information flowing into the brain from the outside world. But today, they've figured out that we respond to what the brain, based on prior experiences, expects to happen next.

Scientists have discovered that the mind is such a powerful instrument, it can deliver literally everything you want. **But you must believe that what you want is possible** ...

This is where visualization works its magic. Seeing is believing!

By programming your brain to expect that something will happen a certain way, you achieve exactly what you anticipate.

How do you create a vision or prosperity board that works? It's simple: Your vision board should focus on how you want, or expect, to *feel*. Because you're aiming for health, happiness, joy and prosperity, you'll *expect* to feel great! So, be sure to evoke these feelings on your prosperity wall.

To create the life of your dreams, focus on your joy. Allow the Universe to give you every good thing you deserve, by being a magnet to them. To magnetize every single thing you desire, you must be a magnet of love and manifest your preferred future by imagining better.

Bring your vision of prosperity into being. It doesn't have to be a wall—it could be a poster board you can move around. Or, as my partner and I once did when visualizing the million-dollar property we dreamed of buying (and later purchased), you can create a manifestation fridge!

14

WONDERFUL WINS

Pursue your dreams with the tenacity of a terrier chasing a ball. Create an inspired intention that would fill you with joy when it's achieved.

It doesn't have to be grandiose and it doesn't have to be related to your career, it may be as simple as losing excess weight that's dragging you down, taking up an interesting hobby, or asking someone out on a date.

Perhaps, it's having the courage to quit the day job you hate and putting all your energy into your creative career, following your heart's desire and starting a purpose-driven business.

Are you lonely? Would a wonderful win be the willingness to be vulnerable and open your heart to love again?

What matters is that your intention is meaningful and will have a tangible impact on your life. It's something you feel you'd get a lift from saying, "I did that. I did the thing I never thought I could."

Or perhaps, it's proving others' limited expectations of you to be wrong.

If you're unfamiliar with setting inspired intentions here's a simple strategy to help you WIN:

. . .

W—What do you want to achieve? Be specific. Make your inspired intention concrete so you can almost see, touch, taste, feel, hear it as being your reality now.

I—Inspiration? What's motivating and inspiring you to win? List as many benefits which will flow when you've achieved your inspired intention

N—Needs. What are the next steps? What do you need to do or put in place to win? What's your success strategy to ensure you stay on track?

S—Sweet success. What riches or rewards will you reap when you've achieved your inspired intention? Reward yourself with a treat each time you achieve something significant on your journey to success. Dangle a grand prize in front of you nose that will further motivate you to persevere.

I've found this simple strategy really helps me create and sustain my vitality. Give it a go and see if it helps you achieve exceptional results too.

15

DREAM BIG

"Dream big," encourages James Patterson, currently the bestselling author in the world. "Don't set out to write a good thriller. Set out to write a #1 thriller."

Patterson, whose father was raised in a poorhouse, knows the power of big dreams and passionate perseverance. His first book was turned down by 21 publishers and won The Edgar for Best First Mystery. He also quit a lucrative legal career because it didn't make him bounce.

Given that science has barely even begun to explore the real potential of the human mind, it's a funny thing how easily we persuade ourselves of its limitations and settle for less.

You've probably caught yourself thinking about a big dream, some inspired course of action, and at some point talked yourself down by saying, "I could never do that!"

Or perhaps you've come up with a bright idea about something and then shelved it because somebody said dismissively, "You can't do that!" or "That's crap."

Or perhaps, as I have so often said to myself before reconnecting with my millionaire mindset, "I can't do this. I can't write this book.

It's too big. Who do I think I am trying to write such a complex book?"

But how do you really know what you are capable of unless you try?

Paulo Coehlo, author of *The Alchemist*, once said: "Know what you want and try to go beyond your own expectations. Improve your dancing, practice a lot, and set a very high goal, one that will be difficult to achieve. Because that is an artist's million: to go beyond one's limits. An artist who desires very little and achieves it has failed in life."

Thinking big demands a long step outside the comfort zone of what you know.

It can feel scary to contemplate stepping out of the space where you feel you know what you're doing and you feel fully in control.

It can feel frightening to explore what it would be like if you were to leave the comfort rut and attempt to climb toward a new summit. You don't know for sure where it will lead. But everyone who's ever made a success of anything started with a big dream.

And you can, too.

Tim Ferris dreams big by adopting and cherishing his beginner's mind. Rather than succumb to the fear of failure, he changes his mindset, and affirms his love of variety and challenge and being a perpetual debutante.

"Think small, to go big" encourages Gary Keller in his book *The One Thing*. "Going small" is ignoring all the things you could do and doing what you should do.

"It's recognizing that not all things matter equally and finding the things that matter most. It's a tighter way to connect what you do with what you want. It's realizing that extraordinary results are directly determined by how narrow you can make a focus."

When you think too big, achieving success can feel overwhelming, time-consuming, and complicated. Calendars can become overloaded and success starts to feel out of reach. So, people opt out and either quit or settle for less.

"Unaware that big success comes when we do a few things well, they get lost trying to do too much, and in the end, accomplish too little," says Keller.

"Over time they lower their expectations, abandon their dreams, and allow their life to get small. This is the wrong thing to make small."

Every extraordinary achievement starts as someone's daydream. Dream big, become audaciously obsessed, and fuel your verve—pursue the vision that sparkles and get ready to bounce!

16

BOUNCE BUDDIES

The simplest definition of bounce buddies is a group of supportive people that share the same values, beliefs, and aspirations.

Your bounce buddies are the ones who always have your back no matter how flat or down you feel. They're the ones that you show your vulnerable, wounded, self-doubting self and they still love and support you unconditionally—worry warts and all.

Your bounce buddies can also help motivate, and reenergize you and cheerlead your successes.

As you've already discovered, sometimes to flourish you need to break free of your current tribe and find one that breathes fresh air into your life, lifts you higher and brings out the best in you. Your best-fit bounce buddies are committed co-creators in one another's mutual success.

Your bounce buddies are a great team of supportive others—whether they be significant friends, partners, or family members, or those found online through wonderful Facebook groups and webinars. They may even be your clients.

I found many of my bounce buddies online when I devoted myself to living and working with passion. We've never met in person, but we stay connected and share success strategies via Facebook, emails and occasionally we link-up on video conferencing calls.

One of my key cheerleaders is my partner, Lorenzo. We got together over lunch on day and bounced some ideas around for this book.

When you choose to step out of limiting thoughts and open your heart to others, you'll find the people who want to share and celebrate the journey with you. You'll find your bounce buddies.

My readers have become bounce buddies by reaching out to me and interviewing me on their podcasts and success summits. Recently, Sheree Clark, a fabulous and influential healthy-living coach based in the US, discovered my book *Mid-life Career Rescue: The Call for Change* and showcased it on American television.

She also included an interview with me in her fabulous "What the Fork" summit. You'll find a link to this interview and the TV clip on my media page at www.cassandragaisford.com/media.

Successful authors and podcasters like Tim Ferris (tim.blog/podcast) and Joanna Penn (www.thecreativepenn.com) found their bounce buddies by following their enthusiasms and passionate purposes to share what they learn with others.

Here are a few ways to find your bounce buddies:

• Scan Facebook for like-minded groups

• Enroll in an online course that sparks your interest or is teaching a skill you'd love to master—they often include a private members group on social media

• Create a Facebook community of your own—show up and encourage others

• Listen to podcasts which inspire you to become the best version of you. Tim Ferriss' podcast is always inspiring http://tim.blog/podcast. I also love Emily Thompson and Kathleen Shannon's Being Boss podcast; Hilary Henderschoott's Profit Boss; and Devi Adea's Spiritual Entrepreneur

• Check out Meetup.com and find a group of like-minded souls to meet up with in person

• Speak from your heart, and reach out to those you love, or feel could help

If you're having trouble bouncing, there are many networks within the community that can assist you. This could be your local Church, the LifeLine Service, or the services offered to the community by your Local Council, e.g., Citizens Advice Bureau.

Your own friends and family could also be a great help if you are willing to listen to their suggestions.

Remember, "A problem shared is a problem halved." Gather a team of supportive or like-minded people who will nourish your burning desire, cheerlead, and support you when you feel flat or overwhelmed and who get a buzz from helping you succeed.

17

SELF-SOOTHE

When you feel flat or worried your default thoughts can veer toward the negative. You may find yourself saying, *'I'm broke. I won't succeed. Everyone is out to get me. I'm lonely. I'm useless.'* Or something else discouraging.

The trouble is, these negative affirmations will become your reality. And you don't want that to happen, do you?

To affirm something is declaring it to be true. an affirmation is also a statement you intend to be true. Listen to your words—are your intentions setting you up for failure or success?

Claim back your power and self-soothe. Harness the power of positive affirmations to convince yourself you'll succeed or get through whatever is troubling you. Create and hold a vision for what you know, or wish, can be true.

"I am the greatest," Muhammad Ali used to say repeatedly. "I said that even before I knew I was. I figured that if I said it enough, I would convince the world that I really was the greatest."

A superhero in and out of the boxing ring Mohammed Ali was a fast-talking world-conquering superhero (1942 - 2016).

Similarly, many people experiencing profound grief or trauma often turn to affirmations for comfort. "All is well. Everything is working out for my highest good," Louise Hay, the author of *You Can Heal Your Life*, used to say. "Out of this situation, only good will come."

As you'll discover later the power of hope is a magical thing.

Affirmations repeated regularly work because they program your mind and activate the part of the brain that acts as a filter—registering what's important to you and screening out what you no longer value.

Another reason affirmations work is that they create a dynamic tension. If what you are affirming has more bounce than what you currently believe, the tension between the two different realities becomes uncomfortable.

To rid yourself of the tension you can either accept the status quo and stop saying the affirmation or raise your reality and bounce higher by making the affirmation and reality match.

Plant your affirmations deeper by framing them emotionally. Instead of, "Obstacles do not bend me", experiment with "I feel strong in the face of obstacles they do not bend me", for example.

Or, "I am joyfully building greater resilience, every day I grow stronger."

These emotion-laden statements engage your heart-center so that deeper, more resilient changes can take root.

Deeper changes creates greater, habitual , instinctive resilience.

18

MAGIC MORNINGS

"If you win the morning, you win the day," says millionaire author, podcaster and polymath Tim Ferriss. Despite his phenomenal success Tim suffers from anxiety and credits a robust morning routine and other health behaviors with giving him more bounce throughout the day.

Ferriss kick-starts his day with 10-20 minutes of transcendental meditation, five to 10 minutes of journaling or Morning Pages, making his bed, and a healthy dose of positive vibes. He also does at least 30 seconds of light exercise. 30 seconds!

"Getting into my body, even for 30 seconds, has a dramatic effect on my mood and quiets mental chatter," Ferriss wrote in his book *Tools of Titans*.

I've followed a similar ritual for years—long before I discovered Tim Ferris. But whenever I am tempted to flag my meditation or my ritual of writing in my journal, I find it helpful to remind myself these are the tools Titans like Tim use to achieve phenomenal results.

Below are just a few of the many *Magic Morning* routines and rituals you can use to prime your day for miracles:

• **Meditation and mindfulness**—enjoy some sacred silence

- **Affirmations**—empower your beliefs with feeling-based reminders of your intentions
- **Goals to go for**—set your priorities, including health and well-being activities (exercise etc.)
- **Inspiration**—journaling, visualization, reading
- **Co-create**—partner with spirit, tap into your Higher Self, evoke the muse…and get ready to create

Importantly, complete these crucial focusing activities *before* you get to work.

I experience many of these activities simultaneously when I meditate, write my Morning Pages, and consult the oracles; and also when I go for a walk in nature, listen to an uplifting audiobook or podcast, or sip my morning coffee.

Ferriss, in a podcast episode, sums up the potency of similar mindful practices: "It's easy to become obsessed with pushing the ball forward as a Type-A personality and end up a perfectionist who is always future-focused.

"The five-minute journal is a therapeutic intervention, for me at least, because I am that person. That allows me to not only get more done during the day but to also feel better throughout the entire day, to be a happier person, to be a more content person—which is not something that comes naturally to me."

I'm not alone in knowing the positive difference daily habits like journaling or taking the time to reconnect with my higher self, makes to my resilience and happiness levels.

Get your day off to a high-vibration start. Choose, develop, and apply your own Magic Morning routines.

19

CONSULT THE ORACLES

Another morning ritual I love is beginning my day being intuitively guided by oracle cards. Not everyone believes in mysticism—but I do. And so do a great many others.

"If you want to be a serious writer or intellectual you can't say you're a mystic because no one will talk to you again," says American author (and professional tarot card reader) Jessa Crispin, slightly tongue-in-cheek.

But, it may surprise you to know that many Titans consult oracles to improve their mindset and boost their productivity and performance.

Subjects such as astrology, psychic phenomena, spirituality, and a fascination with tarot and oracle cards have helped many creative people and successful entrepreneurs overcome doubt, strengthen their beliefs, clarify their direction and find meaning in challenging situations.

As I share in my book *The Art of Success: How Extraordinary Artists Can Help You Succeed in Business and Life,* Coco Chanel found great wisdom, peace, comfort, and healing from oracle cards and an eclectic array of spiritual rituals.

Oracle reader and spiritual adviser Colette Barron-Reid credits this spiritual practice, and others, with saving her life and helping her recover from chronic alcoholism and drug abuse.

"Faith in the guidance of Spirit gives you the courage to take risks because you're assured that whatever happens, a Higher Power is on your side and you will survive," says Barron-Reid.

"Increasing numbers of people are looking to ancient oracles to receive personal guidance because they are not getting the answers and insights they need when they consult the usual sources of psychology and science," she says.

However, there are some highly influential psychologists who do value the wisdom and intuitive guidance that oracles herald.

Of all the psychological theories in the West, that of revered Swiss psychologist Carl Jung stands out as most applicable.

Jung wrote about Tarot on several occasions, seeing it as depicting archetypes of transformation like those he found in myths, dreams, and alchemy.

He described its divinatory abilities as similar to the ancient divination text I Ching, and to astrology. Later in life Jung established a group which attempted to integrate insights about a person based on multiple divination systems including Tarot.

Jung, Crispin, Colette Barron-Reid, and other healers like myself are proud to join many others who invite people to experience a new, or rather old way, of finding hope, courage and comfort to live an inspired, joyful life.

Consider experimenting with oracles and making these, and other spiritual practices, part of your daily bounce ritual.

20

FEAR LESS

As author and filmmaker Michael Moore said, "I want us all to face our fears and stop behaving like our goal in life is merely to survive. Surviving is for game show contestants stranded in the jungle or on a desert island. You are not stranded. Use your power. You deserve better."

So many people let fear limit their potential. They fail before they even try. Fear of success, fear of failure, fear of disappointment, fear of humiliation, fear of losing your relationship—the list goes on. There's a whole swag of fears out there and a host of industries clamoring to feed it. Cultivating fear is big business and the favored official tool for control by oppressive totalitarian agencies and regimes.

Fearful thinking can balloon into anxiety, paranoia, and paralysis.

It takes energy to rise above fear. But you can bounce back. You can reclaim your power—you can pour your energy into people, things and situations that spark joy. You can avoid people and situations that feed your anxiety. Or you can be a stone wall and just let fear bounce off you. Perhaps you may decide to face your fear and remind it you're the boss—what you say, what you want, what you desire goes. Full stop.

As Susan Jeffers, the author of *Feel the Fear and Do It Anyway* so eloquently advised, you can do the thing you fear and the death of fear is certain.

Or, as the Buddhist nun Pema Chodron advises, you can cultivate loving kindness toward your fear.

"Openness doesn't come from resisting our fears but from getting to know them well. We can't cultivate fearlessness without compassionate inquiry into the workings of ego. So, we ask ourselves, 'What happens when I feel I can't handle what's going on? What are the stories I tell myself? What repels me and what attracts me? Where do I look for strength and in what do I place my trust?'"

Cultivate curiosity and consider asking your fear to have a chat with you. Ask, "Fear, what are you wanting to say?" "What do you want me to know?" "Fear, what are you wanting to teach me?" "How will you help me fulfill my highest potential?"

One of my fears is of living in poverty. Mystics have told me it's a fear that I have brought forward from past lives.

As a self-employed business owner who makes her living from creativity, I know that many artists are starving artists. But if I challenge my fear I am reminded that the opposite is also true.

The gift of this fear is the way it fires my determination to succeed. I don't want to fail, and I don't want to surround myself with people or situations that feed my fears.

One of the best ways to overcome this fear of being an impoverished artist is to learn from others who have succeeded. I study their books and oracles of wisdom, I listen to their podcasts and devour their wise words of success, and I pay it forward by sharing what I learn so that other people, like you, may succeed.

Conquering your fears and helping others do the same is a fabulous bounce strategy.

21

MAKE MISTAKES

Conquering failure often requires learning the hard way to reach dizzying heights and allowing room for disappointment.

Julia Cameron, author of *The Artist's Way*, advises aspiring authors to affirm the following, "I am willing to write badly; I am willing to do the work whether it is any good or not; I am also willing to allow brilliance." It's wisdom we can all embrace.

Many people stagnate under the weight of perfectionism or fear of failing because they worry about making mistakes.

It may be challenging, but investing in strategies to create more tolerance and acceptance towards making mistakes will prove liberating. One strategy is to learn from others' misfortune.

With hindsight, sometimes the greatest fortune comes from making the biggest blunders. Here are just a few mistakes that turned out well:

Isabel Allende started her career in journalism and soon found herself offside with people who didn't appreciate her outspoken views. For years she felt under-appreciated—until she decided to tackle her first novel, *The House of the Spirits*.

The novel was named Best Novel of the Year in Chile in 1982, and Allende received the country's Panorama Literario award. *The House of the Spirits* has been translated into more than 37 languages. It was also adapted into a film of the same name starring Jeremy Irons, Meryl Streep, Winona Ryder, Glenn Close, and Antonio Banderas.

Musician Ornette Coleman's mistake led her to be acclaimed as the inventor of "free jazz." She was awarded the MacArthur Fellowship (nicknamed the Genius Award) in 1994 and the Pulitzer Prize for Music in 2007.

"It was when I found out I could make mistakes that I knew I was on to something," she once said.

Walt Disney was fired by a newspaper for lack of ideas. He also went bankrupt several times before he and his brother co-founded Walt Disney Productions, one of the best-known motion picture production companies in the world. Disney's revenue last year was $US45 billion.

Dr. Suess' first children's book, *And to Think That I Saw it on Mulberry Street,* was rejected by 27 publishers. The 28th publisher, Vanguard Press, sold six million copies of the book. He went on to write numerous other books which still sell well today.

Rhonda Byrne's life was at an all-time low. Fifty-five and twice divorced, her father had just died and her career was in crisis.

That was until, acting on an inspired thought, she created the DVD *The Secret* and later produced a book, both of which galloped away to become some of the biggest-selling self-help resources of all time.

At the heart of Byrnes' inspirational series of products is the Law of Attraction.

"Everything in your life is attracted to you by what you are thinking," Rhonda says. "You are like a human transmission tower, transmitting a frequency with your thoughts. If you want to change anything in your life, change the frequency by changing your thoughts."

Refuse to be a victim. Next time you feel you've made a mistake, ask yourself, "How could this work out for my highest good?"

Be gentle with yourself. Sometimes making mistakes heralds a time of new birth and energy. Draw on the lessons you have learned to help you move forward

Notice how you have grown and changed due to everything that has happened. Gather information as you go and be ready for a new adventure. Look for positive signs for successful outcomes in the future.

Buoy your courage and resolve by collecting stories about other people who felt like failures, or were treated harshly by peers, critics, family, and other disbelievers. Collect a file of inspiring stories about mistakes that turned out well.

Follow your inspiration and bounce back from mistakes.

22

FAITH IN YOUR STARS

"Most clients come with financial problems or relationship problems," my friend and astrologer Marianne O'Hagan says. "They come looking for the hope of happiness in the future."

Marianne knows personally and professionally how astrology can help during times of stress and worry. You can read more of her story in *Mid-Life Career Rescue: What Makes You Happy*—including how she started her own business by using her faith in the stars.

"I liked the idea that astrology believes we all are special and have unique gifts. It was at that moment that my love of astrology was born," she says.

As Pam Gregory shares in her fabulous book, *How to Co-Create using the Secret Language of the Universe: Using Astrology for your Empowerment*, many eminent psychologists, including Carl Jung regard astrology as a sacred science. Jung used astrological insights to help diagnose his patients, and as inspiration for his psychological theories of synchronicity and archetypes.

Knowing who you are and what makes you tick, and what doesn't, is truly an empowering and life-changing experience. 'Know thyself' is a maxim that is as true now as it was in ancient times.

I'm a Libra in Western astrology and a Snake in Chinese astrology.

It's true when they say that Libran's love harmony, balance, and beauty. I love it when I receive feedback from readers, saying my book is "beautifully written."

Or, as one person who posted in their review of my first <u>Art of Success</u> book, inspired by Leonardo da Vinci, posted in their review, *"This beautiful book wraps art around business and life and makes each hum with energy and creativity and brings the reader new vitality."*

Google 'best careers' for Snakes and I'm told to avoid careers where I have to work too hard. 'Working hard' to me is doing something I dislike, working with people I don't respect. Working hard is not marching to my own beat. But when I'm working in the passion zone, fulfilling my purpose, now that's a different story.

Whether or not you're a believer in the notion that whatever planets align at the time and place of your birth, can determine your intrinsic strengths, shape your character, relationships and fortunes, there's plenty of helpful data to aid you in your quest for success. Keep an open mind and don't take everything as total gospel.

Go cosmic—gain additional insight about your astrological sign from any of the plethora of books, online resources and personal astrologers. Focus on identifying your strengths, Achilles heel, and best-fit-factors career-wise and in your personal life.

23

CHASE THE LIGHT

What's your default position when things go awry, obstacles challenge your resolve, technology goes belly-up, unforeseen demands on your time derail your plans, or you receive negative feedback?

Does your mood darken? Setbacks are normal foes that you'll meet on the path to success, but how you greet them will determine the outcome.

Keep your thoughts light. You may need to bring out the big guns to wage war against doubt, despair, and other dark, heavy thoughts.

While they're often part of the journey to success, you will need to slay them to stay motivated and optimistic.

Resilient people turn again and again toward the things that create light. They don't ignore the shadows, but they don't allow their mindset to be overloaded by darkness.

Acceptance, optimism, willpower, grit, stubborn determination, and a resolve to persevere are critical skills to cultivate, as is flexibility and the willingness to adapt.

Sometimes when it's all too hard and you need to hibernate, you may temporarily quit. You can take a lesson from nature in this regard.

But as sure as night follows day, and the seasons have their rhythm, if writing is your gift, your purpose, the thing that makes you happy, before long you'll be up and writing again.

Resist complaining and victim talk—it increases toxicity in your mind and body, hampering your progress.

Throw your energy into positivity—strive to engineer and implement solutions, no matter how small.

WHAT MAKES YOU HEALTHY? PRIORITIZE YOUR WELL-BEING

"Realize that every day you have could be the last one. Live fully. Never forget to laugh as much as possible. The best place to start is laughing at yourself.

In all of your free time, be in nature—go to the seaside, forest, mountains, volcanoes, waterfalls.

Try to be happy with the simple things."

WHAT MAKES YOU HEALTHY? PRIORITIZE YOUR WELL-BEING

~ Marina Abramovic, performance artist

24

STRESS LESS

When you are under too much pressure, take too much on and don't take time out, you tend to live your life on overdrive and on the verge of burnout.

When you're stressed you are less effective, make more mistakes, suffer more and are prone to illness.

Very often people turn to "medicine"—chemical highs, alcohol, and prescription drugs—to manage the symptoms.

But the reality is that these only offer temporary relief. They mask symptoms which, left unresolved, can set fire to everything you've worked so hard to achieve.

Fortify your resilience. Stop, take a break, rest, eat well, stay away from negative people, cultivate optimism, exercise, do things you love, play, spend time in nature, experience the quietness of solitude, and experiment with other effective stress management techniques.

Your Beautiful Brain

On a typical day in the brain, trillions of messages are sent and received. The messages that are happy, upbeat messages are carried by the brain's "happy messengers" (scientifically known as the Biogenic

Amine/Endorphin System). Other messages are somber and disquieting. They are carried by the brain's "sad messengers."

Most nerve centers receive input from both types of messengers. So long as this input is balanced, everything runs along on an even keel; however stress causes problems with the brain's happy messengers.

When life is smooth, the happy messages keep up with demand. But when too much stress is placed on the brain, the happy messengers begin to fall behind on their deliveries.

As the stress continues, the happy messages begin to fail. Important nerve centers then receive mostly *sad messages*, and your whole brain becomes distressed and chemically imbalance.

When sad messages overwhelm the happy messages, you can feel overwhelmed by life. You may feel more tired, unable to fall asleep, or to obtain a restful night's sleep. Depression, anxiety, or just feeling unable to cope with life often ensues.

TIP the balance back into your favor by making room for the happy messages! Some simple but effective ways include:

- Noticing something beautiful every day
- Daily appreciation of things you are grateful for
- Taking time to indulge and feed your hobbies
- Being with people who make you feel special
- Laughing
- Doing nothing at all!

Be on guard for the "new normal" —burnout.

"The big topic among successful indie writers in the last six months of 2017 is the possibility of burnout," writes author Kristine Kathryn Rusch on her blog.

"Writers are slowly realizing that the pace they've maintained through the last few years isn't sustainable. Worse, it has become clear through data and anecdotal evidence that the more a writer produces, the more her income rises.

"But that fact, coupled with the fact that incomes have fallen for indies in the past year or so, has given rise to something like panic among the successful indies. They're having to work harder or just as hard to maintain an income that seemed to come easier in 2015.

And you know what? That's normal."

DIVE DEEPER...

You'll find more strategies to manage stress, avoid burnout and build greater resilience in the chapters that follow.

25

BURNOUT BLITZ

"We think, mistakenly, that success is the result of the amount of time we put in at work, instead of the quality of time we put in," says Arianna Huffington, Entrepreneur and Author of *Thrive*.

"One thing I see all the time from people in business, they are quick to neglect their needs, health and time, giving it all to their business," says Vesna Hrsto a Melbourne-based Naturopath, Mind-body Medicine specialist and Life Coach.

"They end up losing their energy and spark, the two things you need to sustain a business. They lose access to new ideas, creativity, plus their health and happiness diminishes ultimately burning out. It's your energy, essence and mojo that got you into your business, you don't want that burning out."

Vesna is intimately acquainted with burnout having crashed in the earlier days of running her business. You'll learn more about her story and her path back to health, and how her experience changed the way she practiced, later in this chapter.

She'll also shares some of her strategies to blitz burnout and maximize your health and well-being in my book, *Mid-life Career Rescue: Employ Yourself*.

But first let's look at what stress and burnout are and how they're defined.

Stress Defined

Stress is most commonly defined as: "A condition or feeling experienced when a person perceives that demands exceed the personal and social resources that the individual is able to mobilize."

Similarly New Zealand's Department of Occupational Safety and Health definition is: "Stress is the reaction people have to excessive pressures or other types of demands placed upon them. It arises when they worry that they can't cope."

In other words, we feel 'stressed' when we don't think we can cope. But there is no stress in a situation until you feel strain.

Biology 101

How you choose to react to stressful events, people and situations is an important point. As is, how you choose to fortify yourself against your body's natural stress response, commonly called the fight or flight response. This is a basic biological survival instinct. When you perceive a threat, your body quickly releases hormones designed to help it survive.

Through a combination of nerve and hormonal signals, your body's alarm system prompts your adrenal glands, located atop your kidneys, to release a surge of hormones, including adrenaline and cortisol. Adrenaline increases your heart rate, and elevates your blood pressure. Cortisol, the primary stress hormone, increases sugars (glucose) in the bloodstream.

Cortisol also alters immune system responses and suppresses the digestive system, the reproductive system and growth processes. This complex natural alarm system also communicates with regions of your brain that control mood, motivation and fear.

These 'stress' hormones are designed to help you run harder and faster—hopefully outrunning whatever is threatening you. Which is great if a lion has you in its sights, but not much good if ten-too-many emails send you over the edge. People can also experience this response when frustrated or interrupted, or when they experience a situation that is new or in some way challenging.

There are very few situations in modern life where the "fight-flight" stress response is useful. Most situations benefit from a calm, rational, controlled and mindful approach. Further on in this book we will look at some techniques to keep this fight-or-flight response within your control.

Burnout Defined

Burnout, also known as General Adaptation Syndrome, refers to the way we learn to 'adapt' to the long-term effects of exposure to stress. When pushed to extremes people have been found to react in three stages:

First, in the Alarm Phase, they react to the stressor.

Next, in the Resistance Phase, they learn to adapt to, or cope with, the stressor. This phrase lasts for as long as people can support their heightened resistance.

Finally, when resistance is exhausted, people enter the Exhaustion Phase, and their ability to resist declines substantially. And if this happens to you, so does your enjoyment of life.

As Mindtools.com notes, "Burnout occurs when passionate, committed people become deeply disillusioned with a job or career from which they have previously derived much of their identity and meaning. It comes as the things that inspire passion and enthusiasm are stripped away, and tedious or unpleasant things crowd in."

Holistic Self-Care

Smart and successful people invest time and energy in holistic approaches to health like meditation, mindfulness, massage, exercise, eating well, reducing alcohol and foods that are low in nutritional value. Also avoiding toxic people and situations, are among other simple and savvy strategies. By increasing the body's coping resources and reducing the likelihood of triggering the stress response, they are better able to avoid overload and are better positioned to blitz burnout.

Meditation, for example, is not just about distracting yourself from stress and pain; it literally changes you at the genetic level, writes Arianna Huffington in her best-selling book, Thrive. "It's the Swiss army knife of medical tools, for conditions both small and large."

Ridding yourself of self-limiting thoughts, controlling your reactions, discovering an inner contact with a creative source, and having more creative insights are just a few of the benefits that can flow from meditation. The whole experience is primarily an experience of wholeness, rightness, and power.

Maintaining Vigilance

However, you still need to maintain vigilance. You can put in a variety of self-care measures; but unless you take significant steps to reduce stressors you may wake up one day so exhausted you literally cannot move.

The road back to health, as Clive a man in his 60's who suffered burnout told me, took over three years, during which time he was unable to work and was forced to rely on the generosity of friends.

When you are your own boss, unless you have cash reserves, or a supportive other, there is no paid sick leave. There may not be anyone urging you to take good care of yourself. This is where your own self-discipline and ability to self-regulate comes in.

Remember—you're in control. You're in charge of yourself and your business. And you're the one that has to be proactive about your own self-care.

You may opt not to take on more and more work when you already feel overloaded, or learn to delegate or outsource responsibilities, or turn down clients who are not aligned with your values, or turn the phone off and go bush for a week!

Whatever you do, know that self-care is an investment in the business of being you. The mental, spiritual, financial, physical and emotional impact of stress and burnout are too costly to ignore.

LISTEN To Your Body Barometer

If you've read my first book in the Mid-Life Career Rescue series, *The Call For Change*, you'll know that the key to managing stress successfully is to heed the early warning signs.

Here are just a few:

- Irritability
- Depression
- Overwhelm
- Fatigue
- Forgetfulness
- Tension
- Moodiness
- Sleep disturbances
- Elevated blood pressure

By nipping your stressors in the bud before they go to seed, you will avoid wreaking havoc with your body, mind, spirit, relationships and your creative business. Ignore then, and they could cost you dearly.

26

PROTECT YOUR MENTAL HEALTH

Jessie Burton, author of *The Muse and The Miniaturist*, powerfully sums up how devaluing your health can sneak up on you and the importance of protecting your health—mentally, emotionally, physically, and spirituality.

Below is an extract from the vivid account she shared on her blog earlier in 2017:

"I looked my mental health in the eye and did not do enough to protect it. I burned out again, I suffered dehydration and a viral infection, but far worse, my anxiety came in huge and truly awful doses and, in the end, I had to cancel a few events.

"I am well aware of the places I had to cancel events, and one day, I hope to make up for that in those places. It wasn't many, but I did feel terrible.

"I truly love having readers, and I did the best I could, a four-month publicity tour, two continents, five events in three days kind of thing, but by the end of September, the scrutiny and analysis, repetition and a sinking of myself led to physical damage and a deep sense of alienation, panic and an indefinable loss.

"The thing I want most to do in the world is write, and I agonized that if writing led to this kind of struggle, then what was the solution?" she asked.

"Balance. That is the solution. And writing, more than talking about writing," she replied.

"It's too late for me to be an Elena Ferrante [an Italian novelist, best known for her *Neapolitan Novels*]. I have thought much about authority, invisibility, how to synthesize the experience of life into fiction in the best ways I can, the ways that feel truest and strongest and will make a reader go with me and say, yes.

"A writer's selfhood vies with her need to make herself invisible, in order to freely inhabit a simulacra of multiple lives in fiction (aka Ferrante), and work without worrying about her own received persona in all of it.

"A published writer has people pay to read the manifestations of her imagination, soul, and heart.

"For me, that remains extraordinary. It will always be the dream transaction for me, but it is also the most exposing, the rawest, unavoidable, supremely important fact in my life that I have battled desperately to understand and get a handle on these past three years.

"It's a rockier path, certainly, knowing you are going to be held publicly accountable, knowing that your personhood will be as relevant to your artifices when it comes to talking about the work.

"I know I'm not alone in this battle and I am grateful to the other writers who have spoken to me about this on the way, sometimes reaching out without me even having to ask.

"My own lack of anonymity when I publish is something I am coming to accept. I handed it over without even thinking about it.

"I made a pact with the kindly devil with my eyes wide shut, but I do not regret it. Having my novels bought and read has been the best thing that ever happened to me.

"Sometimes, however, the things that are best for us are not always the easiest. I do regret my inability to find my pause button, but maybe writing that regret here will enable me to locate that mysterious setting inside myself?

I want to write, and write well, and that's nearly all I ever want to do."

How can you prepare for inevitable success and avoid overload and overwhelm?

What mental health practices would make a tremendous difference to your sustained prosperity?

You'll find a few helpful reminders and strategies in the chapters which follow.

27

REALITY CHECK

As Joanna Penn writes in her book *How to Make a Living with Your Writing*, "A survey in *The Guardian UK* in April 2015 stated that the median earnings of professional authors fall below the minimum wage.

"The bottom 50% of UK authors made less than £10,500 in 2013 (around US $16,000). It's often reported that the average book will sell fewer than 500 copies, which of course, is not enough for a sustainable income. The top 5% are making more than that."

Yes, people do make a living from their writing and their art, a very good living, but the reality is that many people don't. You'll find it a lot easier to manage your stress levels if you start honestly.

Deluding yourself with an excess of sunny optimism and dreams of getting rich quick will increase anxiety, despondency, and despair. Ultimately, you'll be discouraged from persevering with your goal of making an extraordinary living from your creativity—whether this is writing, painting, dancing, photography or any other creative pursuit.

A healthy reality check doesn't need to be a deterrent to building a successful career. Armed with the facts, you can develop a strategy to increase your odds of success.

Pursuing several careers at once might seem crazy, but not only is it a growing trend, for some—especially as they start out— it's the only way to earn money doing what they love.

James Patterson kept his day job as a lawyer and penned crime novels on the side. He now writes in a variety of genres, and has mastered the art of writing short, impactful books which satisfy his voracious readers.

Author C.J. Lyons continued to work as a paramedic while building her career writing thrillers. She said it took seven books before she started to see a regular income stream.

Mary Bly enjoys her salaried position as a tenured professor of English Literature while penning Regency and Georgian romance novels under her pen name, Eloisa James.

Nicholas Sparks was turned down by over 25 agents and was on the verge of bankruptcy when he hit it big with *The Notebook*. The manuscript was sold for 1 million dollars and was quickly made into the movie we all know and love.

J.K. Rowling lived in near poverty as a single mother on benefits and endured similar rejections before she hit the jackpot.

How can you follow your passion and still pay the bills?
You'll find more suggestions to help you finance your career in the section "Slaying Obstacles," and also in my book *Mid-Life Career Rescue: Employ Yourself*.

28

MAINTAIN SOME BALANCE

Leonardo da Vinci once wisely said, "Every now and then go away, have a little relaxation, for when you come back to your work your judgment will be surer. Go some distance away because then the work appears smaller and more of it can be taken in at a glance and a lack of harmony and proportion is more readily seen."

WORKAHOLISM IS an addiction for many passionate people. Others use overwork to medicate their unhappiness in other areas of their life—most commonly dissatisfaction with their relationships.

When you work slavishly, particularly at something you love, your brain releases chemicals called opiates which create feelings of euphoria. No wonder it's hard to step away!

Euphoria stems from the Greek word *euphoría*—the power of enduring easily. But consider what the state of endurance implies. Enduring implies force or strain, or gritting your teeth and bearing it at times. Force or strain with no respite leads to stress, overload, and burnout—robbing you of vital energy and depleting your millionaire mindset.

Many people find when they don't step away from their work they suffer disillusionment, and things that once filled them with passion, including their current writing project, no longer fills them with joy. Resentment builds and relationships with family, friends, and colleagues can also suffer.

Working addictively offers a short-term fix, but lasting happiness needs variety and nourishment. Being with family or friends, engaging in a hobby, spending time in nature, learning something new, helping others, or just being solitary will help you avoid burnout, nourish your brain, heart, and soul, improve your judgment, and restore harmony.

To be truly happy and successful, you must be able to be at peace when you are working and when you are at rest.

Leonardo da Vinci would often take breaks from his work to refresh his mind and spirit. While others claimed that he took too long to finish things, he knew the importance of replenishing his focus to maintain a clear perspective.

Here we are still talking about him over 500 years later.

Leonardo also valued sleep, noting in one of his journals that some of his best insights came when his mind was not working.

Even if you love the work that you do, and think your book is the greatest thing since man launched into space, it's fun to get away from it and have objective-free time to unwind and reset.

When you return to your work, your focus will be surer, your vision refreshed, and your confidence bolder.

When was the last time you truly relaxed? Can you think of a time when you stepped away from your work and when you returned, your mind was clearer, your confidence surer?

Schedule time out—and be firm with yourself. Stay away from anything that feeds your addiction.

29

GO LOW

When life knocks you flat exercise self-compassion and give yourself permission to go low.

It's important to value bouncing low—many times going low is an essential part of your healing process. Remind yourself that grief, loss and the disappointment you feel when you lose someone or something you love are natural and valid emotions.

Similarly, when you suffer a setback it's natural to be hacked off, hurt or sad.

It's difficult to bounce when you feel flat. But you must be true to yourself and allow your emotions to be felt and expressed, or risk them doing a sit-in, and prove unwilling to budge.

The trick is not to stay low. Be watchful and know when a low mood has the potential to cross the threshold into clinical depression.

Your ability to bounce-back will only stay low if you hold it down and don't take proactive action to help elevate your mood. This may be simply talking to someone, sharing your emotions with a friend or a skilled professional like a counselor, Sometimes, medical intervention may be required to help you cope with extreme stress.

Practicing some of the other mood enhancing strategies in this book, or recalling a time where you felt similarly stuck and remembering the things that helped you bounce back, may also help you recover your vitality.

If you're worried that you may be clinically depressed don't be too proud to ask for help.

"You don't have to suffer alone. When Buddha sat and meditated under a tree for his enlightenment was that all suffering will pass. That darkness you feel engulfing you right now may just be the experience that will move you into a new authentic expression of your soul. As day follows night, so will light come after a dark period of the soul.

30

BEAUTIFUL BOUNCE

Your Beautiful Mind

When you feel love, joy, gratitude, awe, curiosity, bliss, playfulness, ease, creativity, compassion, growth, or appreciation, you're in your beautiful mind.

Your beautiful mind is in a stand of transcendence and flow. Your spirit and your heart are aligned, and your best self comes alive. Nothing feels like a hassle, everything feels peaceful. You feel no fear or frustration. You're in harmony with your true essence.

Your Suffering Mind

When you're feeling stressed out, worried, frustrated, angry, anxious, depressed, irritable, overwhelmed, resentful, or fearful, your suffering mind has taken control.

Negative feelings and emotions become the norm, even if you'd prefer they weren't.

As I wrote at the beginning of this book, his Holiness the Dalai Lama reminds us, "Nothing beautiful in the end comes without a measure of some pain, some frustration, some suffering."

As I write this chapter, my partner and I are in the midst of our house renovations. A beautiful tree was too ill to be saved. It was devastating to see it felled. It would have been easy to focus on the ugliness of the clay, and mud and debris its removal has left behind. Instead, I turn my attention to the new vision of what will grow—of the beauty which will come again.

Reframe your uglies. Take back control, find and prioritize the beauties—the things that spark joy, that give you pleasure and bring deep satisfaction to your mind, body and soul.

These may be sensory delights, like the smell of fresh coffee, or freshly cut grass, or a whiff of your favorite perfume. Perhaps a stunning photo or a painting sparks joy, or a fabulous piece of architecture. Or, the vivid blue of a summer sky.

Look for the beauty within things you may associate with ugliness. Acknowledge the pain, frustration and suffering as a rite of passage and find the beautiful to reclaim your bounce.

31

LOOK FOR THE GIFT

Sometimes in life, as with photography, you need a negative to develop the positive. What at the time seemed like a low point can, with hindsight, prove to be the most life-changing and meaningful experience.

A classic and powerful bounce strategy is to reframe setbacks is to look for the treasures they may yield.

In *The Book of Joy,* two great spiritual teachers, the Dalai Lama and Archbishop Desmond Tutu, men who have both known tremendous suffering, encourage us all to look for the gifts contained within adversity. One of these gifts is the opportunity to be reborn.

"When I spoke about mothers and childbirth, it seems to be a wonderful metaphor, actually, that nothing beautiful in the end comes without a measure of some pain, some frustration, some suffering," writes the Dalai Lama. "This is the nature of things. This is how our universe has been made up."

In the same book, the Dalai Lama shares how the gift of being exiled from his beloved Tibet provided the opportunity to give birth to a new way of being and to share his teachings and Buddhist philosophy throughout the world. "Life is suffering," he says. "It's how you react to life that changes your karma", he teaches. "I'm just one human being, but I believe each one of us has a responsibility to contribute to a happier humanity."

It is no coincidence that successful and revered people see the cup half full, look for ways to add more to peoples' lives rather than play the victim, and demand that life treats them more favorably.

"If I had been brought up protected and happy, what the devil would I write about?" says Isabel Allende of her troubled childhood. The gift of her previous unhappiness creates bounce in the lives of millions of readers who are enchanted by her words and are inspired by Allende's tales of passion, courage, endurance, and hope.

3 2

EXPRESS YOURSELF

Creative expression and communicating what you truly feel is one of our greatest freedoms. It a simple, joyful and effective way to inject more bounce in your life.

"I write songs to deal with things I otherwise might not be able to," a young woman once said about her budding music career, hobbies and dreams.

"For me to be happy is about pleasing only my heart and not worrying about what others think," says Interior designer Olimpia Orsini about her magically surreal lair in her home away from home in Rome's bohemian Campo Marzio.

"I love what a camera does," says landscape photographer Alicia Taylor. "It opens up people to connect with you, it can take you on an amazing journey, and probably is the only time I feel I've got the guts to do something is when I've got the camera in my hands. I feel like it's a key to the world."

"Knitting saved my life," the waitress at my local cafe told me recently. She told me how her hobby has provided the ultimate cure for her anxiety, and of the joy she finds in knitting for friends.

Without the anxiety of feeling different, author Isabel Allende, says she wouldn't have been driven to create. "Writing, when all is said and done, is an attempt to understand one's own circumstance and to clarify the confusion of existence, including insecurities that do not torment normal people, only chronic non-conformists."

What do these people all have in common? They harness the power of creative expression to rise above the challenges of life.

Don't get caught up in the classical definitions of an artist when you think about creativity, but you don't have to be an artist, painter or sculptor to be creative. Expressing your thoughts, or imagining what doesn't yet exist and then bringing it into being lies at the heart of creative expression.

You could harness the transformational power of creativity by:
- Imagining what could be
- Dreaming
- Challenging the status quo
- Generating ideas
- Designing new products or services
- Expressing thoughts and feelings that are too big or too difficult to put into words visually

Or doing something else that helps you deal with life and creates joy in your heart.

One of the most liberating features of the creative process is that it triggers moments of vitality and connection.

"The arts address the idea of an aesthetic experience.," says Ken Robinson, an internationally recognized leader in the development of creativity.

"An aesthetic experience is one in which the senses are operating at their peak, when you are present in the current moment, when you are resonating with the excitement of this thing that you are experiencing, when you are fully alive."

Being fully alive is part of the enchantment that creative expression holds. This transformational process connects you to your authentic self. But to free yourself you must act.

As Shakespeare once said, "Joy's soul lies in the doing."

33

CONFLICT HAPPENS

As much as we all like to get on, sometimes conflict is inevitable.

People may feel threatened by your success, they may deliberately try to thwart you, or they may misunderstand your motives and desires. You may be slammed by critical reviews.

Your family and loved ones may resent the time you need to spend away from them. You may feel guilty for wanting more from your life.

As da Vinci said, the noblest pleasure is the joy of understanding. Seek first to understand, and then plan your conflict-handling strategy.

This is a message that British architect Dame Zaha Mohammad Hadid took to heart. "Women are always told, 'You're not going to make it, it's too difficult, you can't do that, don't enter this competition, you'll never win it.' They need confidence in themselves and people around them to help them to get on," she once said.

"Unless you're prepared to die for your work, you're no good," she once said. Hadid was a phenomenal architect, and, in 2004, was the first woman to receive the Pritzker Architecture Prize.

However Hadid's success wasn't achieved without criticism. Her bounce strategy was to remain true to her vision and do what she believed.

Fight for your dreams and sharpen your conflict resolution skills so you can bounce back if people go on the attack.

34

RELATIONSHIP RESCUE

In a universe where "like goes to like" and "birds of a feather flock together," we attract to us that which we emanate.

Everything connects to everything else, especially when it comes to the health of your relationships.

Leonardo da Vinci once said, "Marriage is like putting your hand into a bag of snakes in the hope of pulling out an eel."

Read into this what you will, but the theme is clear. Make good choices and marry well, keep your relationship in good health, or don't marry at all.

Be on guard for relationships that are dragging you down. Sometimes this means investing more time and energy into making things work, or having a bit more patience when people important to you aren't at their best. Take the good with the bad, don't give up too easily, work at it and recognize that nothing is absolutely perfect.

If people try to pull you down, take a step back and explore their motives. Fear is often the culprit. The fear that you may surpass them. The fear that your success will highlight their own regrets. Or the fear that when you succeed you will leave them.

If you can't make things work, professionally or personally, be prepared to quit. Divorce your job, your boss, your partner—anyone who is toxic to your health and happiness.

Getting your head bitten off, or feeling like you're surrounded by a vat of snakes, or being held down, will only deflate your ability to bounce.

35

JOURNAL YOUR WAY TO JOY

Recently, while tackling a mammoth writing project, I talked myself into a bit of a funk. I knew that what I really needed were some positive reminders of my intentions and a way to encourage perseverance.

I recalled a strategy Anne Gracie, a successful romance author, once shared in a newsletter, "I love my writing journal. It's my partner in writing, there for me whenever I need it, my confidant and my supporter and my record of where I've been."

Prior to this, I had noticed anxiety building—as it always does when I don't have a special book in which to purge and reshape my thoughts.

Instead of saying "I quit" and "I am so over this," and retelling the story that allowed for failure, I went online and purchased a beautiful unlined leather-bound sketchbook.

With my gold pen, I wrote empowering and encouraging quotes from other authors who have also struggled to maintain a prosperous mindset while writing an epic book.

Top of my list was Jessie Burton's empowering words, "Always picture succeeding, never let it fade. Always picture success, no matter how badly things seem to be going in the moment."

These words reminded me that I was picturing failure. I was telling myself messages of failure. I was feeling failure.

Jesse Burton, the author of *The Muse and The Miniaturist*, is very inspiring to me because she is so honest about her own battles with mental health—including anxiety.

"In February, I was publicly honest about how difficult it had been to handle, process and assimilate in real time some of the changes in my life. Namely, the strange and wondrous effects of *The Miniaturist*. I wrote about anxiety, my first tentative foray into putting that mental morass into words," she wrote in one of her newsletters.

As Burton highlights, blogging and sharing your thoughts with your fans is another form of cathartic journaling—as is writing a book like this.

To minimize stress and boost your bounce mindset, another form of journaling is writing Morning Pages, a strategy developed by Julia Cameron, author of *The Artist's Way*.

The writing is just a stream of consciousness, writing out whatever you are feeling—good (or what one of my clients calls the "sunnies") or not so good ("the uglies").

"It's a way of clearing the mind—a farewell to what has been and a hello to what will be," Cameron says.

"Write down just what is crossing your consciousness. Cloud thoughts that move across consciousness. Meeting your shadow and taking it out for a cup of coffee so it doesn't eddy your consciousness during the day."

The point of this writing is to work with your subconscious and let it work its magic in the creative, healing process.

Keep a writing journal for specific writing projects. It may not work for you, but you will never know until you try.

Start where you are—commit to a daily practice of writing Morning Pages and journal for self-exploration.

DIVE DEEPER...

You can find out more about Morning Pages here http://juliacameronlive.com/basic-tools/morning-pages/

36

MINDFUL MEDITATION

Our brains never get a break and the results can be increased stress, anxiety, insomnia and if left unchecked, even depression. But there is something you can do—meditate.

Meditation changes brain patterns, soothes and connects you to your Higher Self. It's one of the most powerful bounce strategies you'll ever discover.

"It's the Swiss army knife of medical tools, for conditions both small and large," writes Arianna Huffington, the founder of *The Huffington Post* and author of *Thrive*.

So, what's the buzz? Recent research published in *New Scientist* has revealed that meditation can help to calm people and reduce fear. The research found that regular meditation can tame the amygdala, an area of the brain which is the hub of fear memory.

People who meditate regularly are less likely to be shocked, flustered, surprised, or as angry as other people, and have a greater stress tolerance threshold as a result.

By meditating regularly, the brain is reoriented from a stressful fight-or-flight response to one of acceptance, a shift that increases contentment, enthusiasm, and feelings of happiness.

Here are a few of the many ways a regular meditative practice will help you bounce:

- Decreased stress and anxiety
- Improved focus, memory, and learning ability
- Heightened recharging capacity
- Higher IQ and more efficient brain functioning
- Increased blood circulation and reduced hyperactivity in the brain, slower wavelengths and decreased beta waves (Beta State:13—30Hz) means more time between thoughts which leads to more skillful decision making
- Increased Theta State (4—8Hz) and Delta States (1—3 Hz) which deepens awareness and strengthens intuition and visualization skills
- Increased creativity and connection with your higher intelligence

When Tim Ferriss, who practices transcendental meditation, sat down with more than 200 people at the height of their field for his new book, *Tools of Titans*, he found that 80% followed some form of guided mindfulness practice.

It took Ferriss a while to get into meditation, he says in a podcast episode about his own morning routine. But since he discovered that the majority of world-class performers meditated, he also decided to follow the habit.

His practice takes up 21 minutes a day: one minute to get settled and 20 minutes to meditate.

Ferriss recommends two apps for those wanting some help getting started—*Headspace* or *Calm*.

"Start small, rig the game so you can win it, get in five sessions before you get too ambitious with length," says Ferriss.

"You have to win those early sessions so you establish it as a habit, so you don't have the cognitive fatigue of that practice."

Many people find that meditating for 20 minutes in the morning and 20 minutes at the end of the day yields remarkable benefits.

Regularly take time to focus on the present moment. Make meditating for at least 20 minutes a day part of your daily routine for optimum success and well-being.

37

SLEEP

Are you getting enough sleep? It's hard to bounce if you're sleep deprived and your energy is flat.

"We're suffering a sleep crisis," warns Arianna Huffington, co-founder and editor-in-chief of *The Huffington Post* and author of *The Sleep Revolution: Transforming Your Life One Night at a Time*.

Modern science proves conclusively that if you skip out on sleep you're compromising not just your productivity and efficiency, but also your health and well-being.

More than a third of American adults are not getting enough sleep on a regular basis, according to a February 2016 study from the Centers for Disease Control and Prevention.

Sleeping less than seven hours a day, they report, can lead to an increased risk of frequent mental distress, impaired thinking, reduced cognitive ability, and increased susceptibility to depression.

Lack of sleep also increases the likelihood of obesity, diabetes, high blood pressure, heart disease, and stroke. None of which will aid your quest for happiness and joy.

Getting enough quality sleep helps you maintain your mental and physical health and enhances your quality of life. Getting enough shuteye helps you keep the world in perspective, and enables you to refocus on the essence of who you are. In that place of connection, it's easier for the fears and concerns of the world to drop away.

The next time you're worrying and feeling anxious around bedtime, try one of these simple hacks to relax and quieten your mind enough to fall asleep:

- Enjoy a calming cup of herbal tea
- Listen to soothing music
- Read a paperback novel or book of poems
- Take an aromatherapy bath with lavender and other scented oils
- Or, spend time enjoying your favorite relaxation or meditation practice.

You can also enhance your sleep by turning off all devices at least an hour before you go to bed leaving them outside your bedroom.

If lack of sleep is keeping you awake at night and making you tired during the day, consider reading and applying the strategies in Arianna Huffington's book, *The Sleep Revolution: Transforming Your Life One Night at a Time*.

Be ruthless about prioritizing your well-being. Remind yourself of the benefits that will flow when you enhance the length and quality of your sleep.

38

UNPLUG

Are you permanently attached to your device? Are you suffering from information overwhelm? Does the thought of unplugging from technology send your anxiety spiraling?

What if you miss something? What if….what if…

What if you shut it all down and stepped away for a day, a week, a month, or more?

Setting aside protected time each day for direct interaction with people—or for solitude and meditation without scrolling through social media feeds, or fielding a stream of texts—instinctively feels like a good thing, but it's not always easy.

Take time out to unplug, take a step back, forget about what is expected, forget about what you may be missing, and think about what you may be gaining.

Besides the main benefit of being able to enjoy much more peace and hassle-free, uninterrupted time, here are seven other wonderful and lesser-known upsides you'll notice from making the decision to unplug regularly:

Enhanced relationships. Disconnecting from your perpetual tether to iPhones and laptops can do wonders for your real-world connections. This is a no-brainer, and one that so many people seem to miss. Putting your device away and giving the people around you your undivided attention, rather than your device, tells your family, friends and loved ones that they're important to you.

Increased awareness. When was the last time you were fully aware of the beauty that surrounds you? When you unplug, you blitz major distractions. You become aware of small details in people, things, and places that you never really noticed before.

Clarity. Unplugging reduces brain overload. Technological overstimulation overwhelms your mind, reducing your cognitive reasoning skills.

Improved memory retention and mood. Even just detoxing from technology for one day per week is enough to reboot your brain, which can improve your memory and lift your mood—giving you more bounce.

More brain power. Spending less time being a slave to technological stimulation provides more time to focus on doing activities that can grow your brain cells—such as indulging in an enjoyable hobby, learning a new skill, visiting a new place, having new experiences, or going for a relaxing walk.

Enhanced productivity. Do you really need constant access to your social notifications, Facebook updates, your email inbox, a bunch of tabs open in your web browser and other online distractions, to feel in touch and in control? control?

Accumulating interruptions steals peace of mind and minimizes your ability to get things done. Any time you're interrupted from a work-related task by something from your phone or computer, it can take as long as 45 minutes for your brain to refocus.

Mindfulness. When something interesting starts happening, what's your first reaction? Do you whip out your phone, start snapping photos and begin sharing on social media? Or do you savor the moment and delight in being present in that moment? When you unplug, you force yourself to be more present.

Get to the heart of why you're spending so much time connected to technology. Isolate the benefits and issues, and then make the decision as to whether you need to schedule the time to unplug. As with breaking any addiction, unplugging can be a struggle at first, but the benefits are worth it.

39

AVOID OVER-STIMULATION

Sometimes the best way to bounce is to eat what you don't want, drink what you don't like, and do what you'd rather avoid.

Knock things like coffee, caffeinated drinks and foods, alcohol, and nicotine off your list (or at least limit your intake).

These trigger the production of the stress-related hormone adrenaline—which increases your heart rate, prompts the liver to release more sugar into your bloodstream, and makes the lungs take in more oxygen.

While these things may give you a short term high, in the long run, the result is fatigue and low energy levels. This in turn, leads to a vicious cycle of relying on more stimulants to get you through the day.

The impact of excessive coffee and caffeinated drinks has become such a health-hazard, a new disorder, Caffeine Use Disorder, was recently added to the DSM-V—the tool psychologists, psychiatrists, and other mental-health professionals often refer to prior to making their diagnosis.

Are you addicted to caffeine?

If you've experienced these three symptoms within the past year—you may be in trouble:

- You have a persistent desire to give up or cut down on caffeine use, or you've tried to do so unsuccessfully.
- 2. You continue to use caffeine despite knowing it contributes to recurring physical or psychological problems for you (like insomnia, or jitteriness).
- 3. You experience withdrawal symptoms if you don't have your usual amount of caffeine.

Many of my clients notice reduced levels of anxiety, irritability and depression when they kick the habit. They also report feeling better able to cope with stress, once the coffee habit is culled.

Opt for a natural high. Consider replacing caffeine, alcohol, nicotine and other stimulants with fresh juices, exercise, meditation, or some other activity which makes you feel great and sustains energy. Herbal teas are also healthy, caffeine-free alternatives. Try to drink 6-8 glasses (1.7-2 liters) of water a day to boost energy and flush out toxins.

Less artificial stimulation means more natural bounce.

40

MOOD FOOD

As I shared in my book *Developing a Millionaire Mindset* successful people make their health a priority and regularly tune into their body barometers.

It's tougher to bounce if you lack energy, feel stressed, sluggish, lethargic, or unhealthy. Artificially stimulating your mind, body, and soul won't cut it in the long term.

Many of us take for granted how magnificent and clever our bodies are. But for everything to fire optimally, you need to fuel it with food geared for performance, eat mindfully, and not inhale your meal in a race to the finish.

You are what you feed your stomach—which also feeds your mind. For optimum performance, ensure you're putting smart fuel into your body.

Modern nutritionists and health professionals warn of the perils of over- and under-eating; not eating fresh, seasonal, organic food; and chewing insufficiently.

Diabetes is on the rise. Obesity is an epidemic. Cholesterol and blood pressure are going through the roof. And stress, depression, anxiety, and other mental troubles are all trending upward.

Your gut is also your second brain—a major receptor site of

dopamine, a neurotransmitter that helps control the brain's reward and pleasure centers.

Dopamine helps regulate the feel-good emotions we all need to fuel success. It also regulates movement—enabling you to not only see the rewards of your efforts, but to also take action towards them.

Benefits of healthy eating practices include:

- Increased clarity of thinking
- Better memory
- Healthy body weight
- Increased positive emotions
- Enhanced mental, emotional, and physical health
- Improved mood
- More energy and stamina
- Increased goal achievement
- Better sleep
- Longevity

Avoid extremes—too much sloth makes one prone to gluttony, too much activity overwhelms, and too many vain pleasures taken to extremes are a cause of failure.

As I've already highlighted, too much coffee, for example, increases feelings of anxiety. Too much booze, as you'll discover in the next chapter, can send your stress levels soaring.

When you switch from eating unhealthily to healthily, the difference will be tangibly transformative.

Don't forget to set your self up for a bouncy day by eating a nourishing breakfast. Too many people skip this important start to the day.

At first glance, **porridge** might not seem like the most exciting breakfast on the planet. But it's great for your health and way better than a greasy fry-up. One bowl of porridge contain more fiber than a slice of wholemeal bread and is rich in minerals including copper, iron. and manganese.

It's also been proven to prevent blood sugar spikes, due to the low glycemic index of oats.

. . .

LISTED BELOW ARE some helpful energy-enhancing, mood boosting food tips:
- Eat small but regular meals to sustain energy levels and keep blood sugar levels steady
- Meat and fish contain beneficial amounts of iron, as do green leafy vegetables, dried apricots, lentils and other pulses
- Make sure you get sufficient amounts of B-group vitamins, particularly riboflavin, which converts carbohydrates into energy; vitamin B6 essential for energy metabolism; and vitamin B12, required for forming red blood cells that carry oxygen throughout the body. Useful sources of B-group vitamins include wholegrains, chicken, fish, eggs, dairy produce, pulses, shellfish and red meat
- Help your body absorb more iron by drinking a glass of orange juice once a day with a meal. Vitamin C also helps to boost energy
- Other vital minerals include magnesium, which works with potassium and sodium to ensure the efficient working of muscles, along with zinc, which protects against viral infections that often precede chronic fatigue

Avoid
- Sugary foods, including biscuits, cakes, and chocolate. These also promote short-term energy highs, leading to irritability and lethargy
- Alcohol in large quantities
- Refined carbohydrates foods like white bread, pasta, and rice. These destabilize energy levels by causing a sharp increase in blood sugar levels

IT'S easy to miss meals when you're busy, or stressed, so plan ahead. Your body, mind and spirit will love you back.

41

MINDFUL DRINKING

Many people mistakenly believe drinking alcohol will increase their happiness. But alcohol is a depressant and in large quantities is draining on your body and mind.

Experience may have already taught you that too much booze muddles the mind, ignites aggression, reduces responsiveness, and ultimately depresses.

It's also hard to quit—alcohol is one of the most addictive legal drugs on the planet.

It's also a well-documented neurotoxin—a toxic substance that inhibits, damages, and destroys the tissues of your nervous system.

To bounce, many people limit their drinking or consciously decide not to touch a drop. Keeping their resolve often takes extraordinary willpower.

Author and public speaker Deepak Chopra gave up drinking. "I liked it too much," he once said. Steven King, after almost losing his family and destroying his writing career, managed to quit.

Other people like Amy Winehouse devastatingly never made it. At only 27, she died of alcohol poisoning in 2011.

The risk of suicide also increases for stressed workers who turn to drink. As I've already discussed, alcohol abuse and excessive drinking is a major cause of anxiety and depression, impairs mental reasoning and critical thinking—increasing the likelihood of making tragic and often impulsive choices.

Risking destroying your career, ruining your relationships, sacrificing your sanity, and in the extreme, taking your life, is a massive price to pay for a mistaken belief that to be happy, or to numb your anxiety or cope with stress you need to drink more booze.

Bounce beautifully by exploring your relationship to drink and approaching it more mindfully. Consider, a period of sobriety. Instead of focusing on what you may be giving up, turn your mind to what you may gain—a better, more energized version of yourself.

The many benefits of reducing your alcohol intake, or not drinking at all, include:

- ✓ A stronger ability to focus on your goals and dreams
- ✓ Improved confidence and self-esteem
- ✓ Increased productivity
- ✓ Increased memory, mental performance and decision-making
- ✓ Better control of your emotions
- ✓ Sweeter relationships
- ✓ Greater intuition and spiritual intelligence
- ✓ Authentic happiness

NOT EVERYONE BATTLES WITH BOOZE. Whether you cut back or eliminate alcohol entirely, the choice is ultimately yours. Only you know the benefits alcohol delivers or the success it destroys.

MY BOOK, *Your Beautiful Mind: Control Alcohol, Discover Freedom, Find Happiness and Change Your Life*, has plenty of easy, peasy strategies to help you drink less and create more.

42

JUST ADD WATER

As blood is to your heart, so water is to your body. Our bodies are machines, designed to run on water and minerals. Because we're made up of 72 percent of water, it's vitally important for every bodily function.

Insufficient water intake and low consumption of fruit and vegetables can present significant health challenges.

Too much coffee, alcohol, or other diuretics (which increase the amount of water and salt expelled from the body as urine) can also rob your mind and body of energy and vitality.

When you're dehydrated, your thoughts become muddled, anxiety can loom, and you'll feel tired, irritable, unmotivated, and generally lackluster.

In addition to drinking H2O, many people also find gazing upon or immersing themselves in a body of natural water promotes a positive mindset.

It's no coincidence that most millionaires have houses overlooking water.

I love to bath in the hot mineral waters at Ngawha Springs in the far north of New Zealand. Local Maori have long known of the therapeutic properties of bathing in its waters. Even if I feel low, I always emerge feeling great, and my energy and health are always instantly restored.

Create more energy and drive by flushing toxins from your body as well as increasing your connection with water. Some simple, but effective, strategies include:

- Drinking at least eight glasses of purified water a day
- Reducing alcohol and coffee
- Consuming more fruits and vegetables—as close to raw as possible
- Splash water on your face whenever you're feeling overwhelmed. Cold water steps up circulation, making you feel invigorated
- Swim in the sea or a lake, or bathe in hot mineral water— either in a natural spring or by adding Epsom Salts (a mineral compound of magnesium and sulfate) to your bath.

43

YOGA

Yoga, relaxation, and mindfulness practices work behind-the-scenes to help lower the stress hormone cortisol.

Just two 90-minute classes a week is enough to notice an improved stress response, even in those who report being highly distressed, according to research on yoga and meditation coming out of Germany. Study participants noted a decrease in stress, anxiety, and depression.

I came across the following quote, source unknown, and it seems to summarize the key benefits of yoga—flexibility...in body, mind, and spirit: "Blessed are the flexible, for they shall not be bent out of shape."

Yoga classes don't have to be difficult. They can vary from gentle and soothing to strenuous and challenging; the choice of style tends to be based on personal preference and physical ability.

Hatha yoga is the most common type of yoga practiced in the United States and combines three elements: physical poses, called *asanas*; controlled breathing practiced in conjunction with asanas; and a short period of deep relaxation or meditation.

"Available reviews of a wide range of yoga practices suggest they can reduce the impact of exaggerated stress responses and may be helpful for both anxiety and depression. In this respect, yoga functions like other self-soothing techniques, such as meditation, relaxation, exercise, or even socializing with friends," says an article posted by Harvard Medical School.

"By reducing perceived stress and anxiety, yoga appears to modulate stress response systems. This, in turn, decreases physiological arousal — for example, reducing the heart rate, lowering blood pressure, and easing respiration. There is also evidence that yoga practices help increase heart rate variability, an indicator of the body's ability to respond to stress more flexibly."

Researchers at the Walter Reed Army Medical Center in Washington, D.C., are offering a yogic method of deep relaxation to veterans returning from combat in Iraq and Afghanistan. Dr. Kristie Gore, a psychologist at Walter Reed, says the military hopes that yoga-based treatments will be more acceptable to the soldiers and less stigmatizing than traditional psychotherapy. The center now uses yoga and yogic relaxation in post-deployment PTSD awareness courses and plans to conduct a controlled trial of their effectiveness in the future.

Here are a few of the many reported benefits of yoga:

- Improvements in perceived stress, depression, anxiety, energy, fatigue, and well-being
- Reduced tension, anger, and hostility
- Reduced headaches and back pain
- Improved sleep quality
- Improved breathing and deeper relaxation

"*Samskara saksat karanat purvajati jnanam.* Through sustained focus and meditation on our patterns, habits, and conditioning, we gain knowledge and understanding of our past and how we can change the patterns that aren't serving us to live more freely and fully." ~ Yoga Sutra III.

. . .

Nurture your body and soul with regular yoga sessions.

44

BREATHE DEEPLY

In a state of joy and relaxation, you breathe in a deep circular pattern, your heart comes into coherence, and you begin to produce alpha brain waves, giving you access to your own natural tranquillizers and antidepressants.

But under stress your breathing is reversed. Instead of breathing slowly and deeply, your breathing tends to become shallower and more rapid. During times of extreme stress, you can forget to breathe at all!

You may even hyperventilate—breathing in an abnormally rapid, deep, or shallow pattern. You will exhale too much carbon dioxide, and as the level of carbon dioxide in the blood drops, the blood vessels narrow, allowing less blood to circulate. If too little blood reaches your brain, you'll become dizzy and may faint.

Calcium in the blood also decreases, causing some muscles and nerves to twitch. The twitching may result in a tingling or stabbing sensation near your mouth or in your chest. These symptoms include a tight feeling in the chest, as though your lungs cannot receive enough air.

This sensation leads to faster and deeper breathing. The heart may begin to pound, and the pulse rate may rise. Experiencing these symptoms will increase anxiety in some people, which can make the condition worse.

If this happens to you, or you have forgotten how to breathe, try this: breathe in deeply for a count of four, and exhale—slowing for a count of eight. Repeat 10 times. Notice how quickly your body and mind relaxes. Try this anywhere, anytime you notice feelings of stress returning, and beat the stress response. Or tap into a meditation or yoga class for enhanced breathing practice with the added benefit of a mind-body makeover.

Remember to breathe! Breathing deeply can evoke a state of calm and perspective during times of stress, allowing you to cope more effectively and bounce back from setbacks.

45

GET OUTSIDE

It's hard to bounce when you're suffering from low mood. Very often a lack of outside time is the culprit. You're like a flower—you need at least 20 minutes of sunlight every day just to make your hormones work effectively and enable you to blossom to your fullest potential.

To feel and behave normally you need to be exposed to full-spectrum daylight on a regular basis. Medical research suggests some people need as much as two hours a day of sunlight to avoid Seasonal Affective Disorder.

Combine outside time with exercise like walking and not only will you get the light you need, but you'll also recharge your batteries.

Walking outside can also help you gain a new perspective on a troubling situation. When you go outside and take a walk, you increase the electrical activity in your brain, and you breathe negative ions and see in three dimensions.

All this helps you see with fresh eyes the things which are worrying you. Often you'll find that things are not as bad as they first appear, or discover a relatively simple solution.

Monitor how much time you spend indoors. Bounce away from habits that so many people have, like spending too many hours inside in front of two-dimensional computer monitors and TV screens, and then topping off a 12-hour day at work by trying to read themselves to sleep on their Kindle. These are all two-dimensional visual activities, which seldom spark joy.

Let mother earth, the sea and the infinite sky boost your mood. Get outside and allow the sun and outside energy to lift your spirits. Schedule regular fresh air time. Improve your breathing, and take a brisk walk to increase your oxygen levels.

46

MOVE!

Many people lead sedentary lives, but the most successful ones praise the benefits of exercise. Many use their exercise as a time to reset and plan.

Vitamin D sufficiency, along with diet and exercise, has emerged as one of the most important success factors in human health.

During times of low mood or stress you can become lethargic. Convincing yourself that you don't even have the energy or time to exercise can increase feelings of depression and irritability.

Discipline yourself to go out and get some fresh air—ideally somewhere not too frenzied.

Combine brisk walking with deep breathing to boost your energy levels, short-term memory, and state of mind.

When your breathing is calm and steady, your body is in a nurtured state which helps strengthen your immune system. This will help you ward off colds and snuffles.

Numerous studies have shown that exercise promotes the production of positive endorphins, which play a key role in making you feel better about yourself and your capacity to cope.

In the one-sided state of depression, there is very little electrical activity in the brain. A person on a stationary bike has more electrical activity in their brain than a person watching an educational video. The truly depressed person will have such low electrical activity that making basic decisions, including the mood-enhancing decision to exercise (even just a little), becomes very difficult.

Researchers also confirm there is a strong link between breathing, outside energy, and beneficial brainwave patterns. This may explain why so many people say that walking is their meditation—clearing their minds, and allowing space for good ideas to flourish.

Getting up and moving, embracing the flow of 'chi' in your entire system will enable you to activate both hemispheres of your brain – bringing a new perspective as well as greater tolerance to life's stressors.

"It's not that I am thinking but I am in a kind of trance, totally connected with the present moment," Paulo Coelho says. When he returns to his work, his mind is clear and he is more powerfully connected to source energy.

Listen to your body barometer when it tells you to exercise more and sloth less.

Commit to a regular exercise regime and a healthier diet. Be consistent so that changes easily fall into place and become life-affirming habits.

47

STEP AWAY

Workaholism is an addiction for many passionate people. Others use overwork to medicate their unhappiness in other areas of their life—most commonly dissatisfaction with their relationships.

When you work slavishly, particularly at something you love, your brain releases chemicals called opiates which create feelings of euphoria. No wonder it's hard to step away!

Euphoria stems from the Greek word *euphoría*—the power of enduring easily. But consider what the state of endurance implies. Enduring implies force or strain, or gritting your teeth and bearing it at times. Force or strain with no respite leads to stress, overload, and burnout—robbing you of vital energy and depleting your millionaire mindset.

Many people find when they don't step away from their work they suffer disillusionment, and things that once filled them with passion, including their current writing projects, no longer fills them with joy. Resentment builds and relationships with family, friends, and colleagues can also suffer.

Working addictively offers a short-term fix, but lasting happiness needs variety and nourishment. Being with family or friends, engaging in a hobby, spending time in nature, learning something new, helping others, or just being solitary will help you avoid burnout, nourish your brain, heart, and soul, improve your judgment, and restore harmony.

To be truly happy and successful, you must be able to be at peace when you are working and when you are at rest.

Leonardo da Vinci would often take breaks from his work to refresh his mind and spirit. While others claimed that he took too long to finish things, he knew the importance of replenishing his focus to maintain a clear perspective.

Here we are still talking about him over 500 years later.

"Every now and then go away, have a little relaxation, for when you come back to your work your judgment will be surer. Go some distance away because then the work appears smaller and more of it can be taken in at a glance and a lack of harmony and proportion is more readily seen," he once said.

Leonardo also valued sleep, noting in one of his journals that some of his best insights came when his mind was not working.

Even if you love the work that you do, and think your current obsession is the greatest thing since women were allowed to vote, it's fun to get away from it and have objective-free time to unwind and reset.

One of my author friends shared recently how she was feeling totally overwhelmed and close to burnout. To sustain her life, and her career, she's promising herself a reward for all her long hours—three-months off over winter. She's planning to go on a retreat, somewhere warm, maybe the Bahamas or Mexico.

"The whole point of living the creative life is to enjoy it, right?! I'm coming to grips with that mindset," she wrote to me.

Schedule time out—and be firm with yourself. Stay away from anything that feeds your addiction.

When you return to your work, your focus will be surer, your vision refreshed, and your confidence bolder.

48

REST

When your stress levels are high and you get depressed, angry, tense, and lethargic or begin to experience tension headaches etc., that should be a very simple biofeedback signal that need to stop, re-evaluate your choices and take some time out.

Sometimes this can be easier said than done. In our overachiever, overstimulated society, where many people spend more hours every week with their eyes riveted to their iPhone, instead of spending quality time on their own or with family and friends, the whole concept of stopping and resting to restore ourselves seems unusual. But resting to replenish is essential to well-being.

We're pushing ourselves all day long with energy that we don't have. The most common complaint people take to the doctor for is fatigue. Research conducted by a company helping people suffering from adrenal fatigue claims that 80% of people don't have as much energy as they'd like to have.

"It's because we're pushing and using caffeine, sugar and energy drinks and nicotine and stress for energy rather than running on our own energy."

Long-term stress and long-term cortisol will literally alter a person's hormonal profile.

Rest allows the adrenal glands to restore, enabling cortisol levels to return to normal. Long-term stress and long-term cortisol overload can lead to adrenal fatigue and burn-out, altering your hormonal profile, and making it more difficult to return to the real, inspired, happy and creative you.

Give yourself permission to take time every day and every week to have fun, rest your mind and rest your body.

49

MASSAGE

One of my favorite ways to rest is to go for a massage. But, so many people mistakenly think massage is an indulgence rather than a health-behavior.

Some of the many benefits of massage include reduced stress and higher levels of neuroendocrine and immune functioning—which means better hormonal balance and more immunity to disease and illness.

Some studies also suggest that a one-hour massage results in benefits equivalent to a 6 hour sleep.

Sounds good to me, especially when I'm feeling fatigued.

If getting naked isn't your thing, consider an energy healing treatment with a trained Reiki practitioner.

Reiki is a Japanese word. **Rei** means *universal transcendental spirit* and **Ki** stands for *life energy*. Hence, the word carries the sense of universal life energy. Many scientific minds, as well as sage healers, have believed throughout the years that the universe is filled with this invisible life energy, and that the life and health of all living beings is sustained by it.

Increasing evidence suggests that there does exist a superior *intelligent force* which contains all creation and out of which all life arises.

The energy of this force pervades all things and this is the energy that flows through our hands in concentrated form when we treat with Reiki.

Reiki healing is the ancient art of "hands on healing" and offers a natural and holistic approach to mental, emotional, physical, and spiritual well-being.

You don't have to believe in any religion or be particularly spiritual to benefit from Reiki. It's an inclusive, non-religious form of healing and safe for everyone.

When I was experiencing a huge period of stress, I gained so much immediate benefit from my Reiki treatments that I decided to learn this beautiful healing technique. Recently in Bali, I completed my master level training.

You don't have to be Reiki-trained to live by the principles developed by Reiki founder Dr. Mikao Usui: "Just for today do not worry. Just for today do not anger. Honor your parents, teachers and elders. Earn your living honestly. Show gratitude to everything."

Put more fuel in your tank and **give** yourself the gift of a therapeutic massage or Reiki treatment.

50

LAUGH AND PLAY

Laughter, humor and playtime are great tonics during stressful times. Taking yourself or your life too seriously only increases stress. When you learn to laugh despite your difficulties, you light up the world.

"When people just look at your face," the Dalai Lama said to the Archbishop Desmond Tutu in *The Book of Joy*, "you are always laughing, always joyful. This is a very positive message. It is much better when there is not too much seriousness. Laughter, joking is much better. Then we can be completely relaxed."

Laughter triggers the release of endorphins, your brain's feel good chemicals, setting off an emotional reaction which makes you feel better.

"Discovering more joy does not, I'm sorry to say, save us from the inevitability of hardship and heartbreak. In fact, we may cry more easily, but we will laugh more easily, too," says Archbishop Desmond Tutu.

"Perhaps we are just more alive. Yet as we discover more joy, we can face suffering in a way that ennobles rather than embitters. We have hardship without becoming hard. We have heartbreak without being broken."

You may not feel like it, but give laughter a go. Watch a funny movie, stream a stack of whacky comedies, go to a comedy show, or watch a video on YouTube. Hang out with people who know how to have a good time, go to a Laughing Yoga class, or ask someone to tickle you!

Inject some more laughter and playfulness into your life.

Playfulness is bounciness at its best. Cultivate your inner child. Act up a little, goof-off, experiment, relax and detach—if you find yourself in trouble, smile.

BENEFITS OF PLAY INCLUDE:

- Increasing your productivity
- Boosting your creativity and problem-solving skills
- Reducing stress, anxiety, and depression
- Improving your relationships and connections with others
- Bringing more balance, fun, lightness and levity into your life
- Diminishing your worries

As play researcher and psychiatrist Stuart Brown says in his book *Play: How it Shapes the Brain, Opens the Imagination, and Invigorates the Soul*, "A lack of play should be treated like malnutrition: it's a health risk to your body and mind."

The Dalai Lama agrees. "I met some scientists in Japan, and they explained that wholehearted laughter—not artificial laughter—is very good for your heart and your health in general."

Some of the many ways I play include: "wagging" work sometimes and taking my inner child on a playdate to the movies, going for a massage, or indulging in my hobbies and playing with my paints. Listening to music from the 70s is also playful and brings levity. While travelling internationally recently, I watched the Disney children's movie *Frozen*. I haven't laughed so much in years.

I also love reminding myself of the magic of writing and reading. As novelist Caroline Gordon once wrote, "A well-composed book is a magic carpet on which we are wafted to a world that we cannot enter in any other way."

Author Deepak Chopra confirms the power of lightening up, "When we harness the forces of harmony, joy and love, we create success and good fortune with effortless ease," Chopra says.

51

SMELL YOUR WAY TO HAPPINESS

Along with your skills and capabilities, it is your state of mind that determines how happy you will be.

There are many ways to empower your mind—working with essential oils is one of the most effortless. The sense of smell is the most basic and primitive of all our senses and is of vital importance to your well-being.

The process of smelling is called olfaction and is incredibly complicated, taking place in several areas of the brain including the limbic system which itself has approximately 34 structures and 53 pathways. The limbic system is linked to sensations of pleasure and pain, and emotions— both positive and negative, including fear and confidence, sadness and joy and other feelings that can either erode or boost productivity and prosperity.

The simple truth is that even if you are unaware of the power of smell, aroma affects your mood.

Scientists now believe that all our emotions are the result of neurochemicals such as noradrenaline and serotonin being released into the bloodstream, and mood swings are thought to be a result of these influences, particularly when they are in the extreme.

Given these facts, it's not hard to see how essential oils can help balance and influence our thoughts, feelings, and behaviors.

"Feeling educated about essential oils is such an empowering experience because there are so many different oils you can work with," writes Clinical Aromatherapist Andrea Butje in her book, *The Heart of Aromatherapy: An Easy-to-Use Guide for Essential Oils*.

"They all offer the nourishment of the plant they are distilled from in a single drop, and education helps you understand which oils to reach for at which times. Nature works holistically…and so do we."

As I share in my book, *The Art of Success: How Extraordinary Artists Can Help You Succeed in Business and Life*, Coco Chanel knew the alchemical potency of flowers and plants. She surrounded herself with nature's elixir and amassed a fortune from the essential oils which helped make her perfume Chanel N°5 famous.

The transcendent alchemy of the potions that went into the Chanel N°5 formula was not left to chance. Grieving after her lover Boy Chapel's death, Coco drew upon the essences of jasmine, ylang ylang, vetiver, and other restorative scents to imbue Coco's Chanel N°5 with hope, healing, and the sensual confidence that love lost would be found again.

Aromatherapy, using the scents of plants and flowers, is one of many ancient remedies validated by modern science today. It's the Swiss army knife of all things healing—physically, mentally, spiritually, and emotionally.

There are so many different essential oils that can help you. Here are a few essential oils and natural therapeutic remedies to help increase your alertness and refresh and uplift your mind, body, and spirit:

- Laurel Essential Oil: Motivates people who lack energy or confidence. It also strengthens the memory and helps maintain concentration, especially during prolonged tasks
- Rosemary Essential Oil: Instills confidence during periods of self-doubt and keeps motivation levels high when the

going gets tough. It is also said to help maintain an open mind and to make you more accepting of new ideas.
- Cardamom Essential Oil: Stimulates a dull mind, dispels tensions and worries, and nurtures and supports the brain and nervous system. Many people find it of great support during challenging times.
- Peppermint Essential Oil: With its refreshing scent peppermint works like a power boost for your fatigued mind, making you feel sharper and more alert.

Alertness:

- Ginger 6 drops
- Grapefruit 5 drops
- Juniper Berry 4 drops
- 15 ml of a carrier oil

Energizing:

- Lavender 8 drops
- Lemon 2 drops
- Orange 6 drops
- Rosemary 4 drops

AROMATHERAPY FOR EMOTIONAL WELL-BEING

The use of essential oils for emotional well-being is what is often first thought of when someone thinks of the term "aromatherapy."

Although aromatherapy should not be considered a miracle cure for more serious emotional issues, the use of essential oils can assist, some-times greatly, with certain emotional issues.

For example, lavender is a well-known mild analgesic, useful for healing headaches, wounds, calming the nerves, insomnia, and mild depression.

Rosemary, on the other hand, is a mild stimulant and is used to treat physical and mental fatigue, forgetfulness, and respiratory problems among other ailments.

STRESS-RELIEVING BLENDS

THESE BLENDS STATED below can help during times of stress. When selecting and using oils, be sure to follow all safety precautions and remember that aromatherapy should not be used as a substitute for proper medical treatment.

Blend 1

- Three drops Clary Sage, one drop Lemon, one drop Lavender

Blend 2

- Two drops Romance Chamomile, two drops Lavender, one drop Vetiver

Blend 3

- Three drops Bergamot, one drop Geranium, one drop Frankincense

Blend 4

- Three drops Grapefruit, one drop Jasmine, one drop Ylang Ylang

DIRECTIONS:

1. Select one of the blends shown above.
2. Choose how you'd like to use the blend and follow the directions below:

DIFFUSER BLEND

Multiply your blend by four to obtain a total of 20 drops of your chosen blend. Add your oils to a dark colored glass bottle and mix well by rolling the bottle in between your hands. Add the appropriate number of drops from your created blend to your diffuser by following the manufacturer's instructions.

BATH OIL

Multiply your blend by three to obtain a total of 15 drops of your chosen blend.

BATH SALTS

Continue by using the five drops, blend with Bath Salts.

MASSAGE OIL

Multiply your blend by two to obtain a total of 10 drops of your chosen blend.

AIR FRESHENER

Multiply your blend by six to obtain a total of 30 drops of your chosen blend.

INVESTIGATE THE POWER OF AROMATHERAPY. What scents imbue you with confidence? Courage? Productivity? Sharpen your most potent tools—your heart and your mind. Become a perfumer—experiment with essential oils until you find a winning blend.

Create your own success blend, or have an expert create one for you. Beginning with how you want to feel is a good place to start.

52

BOUNCE WITH COLOR

Color has a profound effect on us at all levels - physical, mental, emotional, and spiritual.

We are in a world where color dominates our lives, from reading signs on the road to identifying ripe fruit by its color.

Color affects our moods. Blue is calming. Red can make us tense. We use color every day in our lives without even appreciating it.

Decide on the mood you want to be in and choose a color that makes you feel that way. For example, if you want to feel calm, you may choose green or blue.

Remember that color is individually perceived, so choose what works for you. On some days red may make you feel energized, on others it may fuel feelings of anger or aggression.

You may want to wear your bouncy color in your clothes, or just to have a small dose of color nearby to prompt these feelings along – for example, it may be some color on your desktop or on a prompt card by your PC or in your wallet.

Wearing color also sparks joy in others. As a shop assistant recently said to me, "You have just made my day with how pink and sparkly you are."

The right color can also empower you and give you the courage and strength of a warrior. During a particularly stressful time in my life, and that of my daughter's, I had to rescue her from the clutches of a former patched gang member. It was also like a scene in a movie. I wore white. White lace, in fact. Elegant, chic, peaceful—and regal. He wore black. Dark. Low. Fierce.

Before I arrived to meet him, I visualized white light all around me. I prayed for help from my angels and guides, and importantly I sent love to this wounded, but dangerous man. Love and the white light won. He surrendered my daughter back to me—something this dominating, controlling man had previously refused to do.

What colors feed your courage? What hues boost your resilience? Surround yourself with colors that empower you and spark joy and banish those that don't.

53

ALWAYS BOUNCE BACK

Resilient people are flexible, they bend with the winter gales and arc with the summer breeze. When the fury of a hurricane knocks them down, they get back up again—and it's the getting back up that elevates your bounce.

When you get back up life will reward you for your efforts. It may not be instant, it may not happen the very same day, but it will happen. That's what you must keep believing in.

What is certain is that unless you put in the energy nothing good will happen at all.

Taking empowered action may result in better health, improved relationships, improved finances, and respect and admiration from people for your courage, tenacity and perseverance.

"You're like a cat with nine lives," a friend once said to me, following a particularly traumatic breakup. "You always land on your feet."

I've been a single mother, receiving no financial support from my daughter's father. I survived a very challenging childhood. I've experienced the most horrific workplace bullying. I've been physically assaulted, intimidated and threatened. And I've also had to rescue my daughter from the fists of a violent man.

I've had to face my fears of public speaking, criticism, failure and standing out. I've had to empower my mind, body and spirit with new tools—many of which I have shared in this book. Meditation, mind power, spiritual-based practices, nutrition, counseling, reading self-empowerment books, like this one—and more.

I've worked hard to cultivate courage, optimism and resilience. In fact, one lady I worked with once said, "You know what your problem is Cassandra? You're too happy."

I knew the bigger problem, the one that lurked inside, was a tendency to be too sad. I decided what I wanted more of.

Happiness.

Feeling sad, staying down,—well, it just doesn't spark joy.

I know what it's like to feel so low that you don't think you can go on. I know what it's like to contemplate ending your life. I know a great many people feel the same. And it's these people, the ones with the will to survive who work everyday, as the Dalai Lama urges, to cultivate happiness, optimism, a resilient mindset—and to pay it forward by helping others.

As Robbie Williams once sang, "I get knocked down, but I get back up again. You're never gonna keep me down."

And you can, and will too.

WHAT MAKES YOU PERSERVERE? SLAYING OBSTACLES

"Obstacles cannot crush me; every obstacle yields to stern resolve."

~ Leonardo Da Vinci

54

REAL RESILIENCE

Ups and downs, highs and lows, troughs and peaks are a rite of passage for many creatives.

The fickleness and unpredictability of fluctuating income, the extremities of your emotions, the quick and ready insights you experience, the acute sensitivity with which you feel almost everything, can make you vulnerable.

But it doesn't have to be this way. By strengthening your inner power, your ability to handle stressful situations, and your skill in persevering after setbacks threaten to fell you, you'll develop resilient grit.

Grit comes in many shapes and sizes: courage, courageousness, bravery, pluck, mettle, backbone, spirit, steel nerve, resolve, determination, endurance, guts, spunk, tenacity—and the strength of vulnerability. Add the flexibility and determination of resilience and you'll have a winning combination.

Resilience is that indefinable quality that allows some people to be bowled over by life and re-emerge stronger than ever. Rather than letting setbacks overcome them and drain their resolve, they find a way to rise from the ashes.

Psychologists have identified some of the factors that will make you more resilient, among them a positive attitude, optimism, the ability to regulate emotions, and the ability to see failure as a form of helpful feedback.

Life as a creative will keep throwing you curveballs— haters or disenchanted readers may post scathing reviews, your books may not sell in the quantities you hoped, an editor or agent may betray you. Or perhaps life threatens to drown you in a deluge of seemingly never-ending hassles—family dramas, environmental mayhem, world affairs, or some other distraction.

As Buddhists say, life is suffering—it's how you react to a setback that counts. We choose our attitude via our thoughts. "With our thoughts, we make the world," Buddha once said.

Many of the strategies I've shared with you in this book will help you develop a millionaire mindset and with it more staying power, passion, perseverance, and grit.

Mindfulness techniques, avoiding excessive alcohol consumption, keeping your thoughts positive, surrounding yourself with a vibe tribe of positive supporters, getting rid of toxicity (friends, family, or stinkin' thinkin'), meditating, exercise, reprogramming your subconscious beliefs, and other strategies are just some of the things you've learned in *The Happy, Healthy Artist*.

But, as someone said to me recently, "Life's hard enough without having to do all this 'feel good' stuff." That, dear reader, comes down to choice. Your choice.

Personally, I don't want to live, nor end my life, as F. Scott Fitzgerald did—a poor drunk who felt like a failure and only found success when he was dead.

I don't want to lie in my grave like Amy Winehouse, a dead, tortured "success" at 27. According to hypnotherapist Marisa Peer, who said Winehouse had cancelled an appointment with her, she had refused to change her mindset. What a sad and tragic waste of talent and potential.

It's not easy to overcome many of the things that hold you back. But you can do it—if you're willing to be strong and fight for your dreams. Within many of us lies an innate seam of strength, which, when mined skilfully, will produce an endless source of pure gold.

As author and filmmaker Michael Moore said, "I want us all to face our fears and stop behaving like our goal in life is merely to survive. Surviving is for game show contestants stranded in the jungle or on a desert island. You are not stranded. Use your power. You deserve better."

I took these words to heart many years ago. Anxiety and depression run in my family—as does a tendency to place a stop-cap on dreams. My grandmother grew up in foster care. Her father murdered a man. I'm sure that her upbringing had an impact on my mom, and in turn, my mom's ability to give me the love I craved as a child.

My dad was dumped in a boarding school when he was only four. He never knew his father, and only found out when he was in his 70s that he had a sister. Growing up, he never experienced a hug or knew true affection.

Like Amy Winehouse and so many others with wounded childhoods, I never felt loved. I've worked hard to overcome the wounds of my childhood.

You should, too. Your past doesn't need to stop you.

"A lot of people feel like they're victims in life, and they'll often point to past events, perhaps growing up with an abusive parent or in a dysfunctional family," writes Rhonda Byrne in *The Secret*.

"Most psychologists believe that about 85 percent of families are dysfunctional, so all of a sudden you're not so unique. My parents were alcoholics. My dad abused me. My mother divorced him when I was six . . . I mean, that's almost everybody's story in some form or not," she says.

Author Jack Canfield also speaks to this point: "The real question is, what are you going to do now? What do you choose now? Because you can either keep focusing on that, or you can focus on what you want. And when people start focusing on what they want, what they don't want falls away, and what they want expands, and the other part disappears."

In hindsight, you will see your life experiences as a gift. As Isabel

Allende once said, "Without my unhappy childhood and dysfunctional family, what would I have to write about?"

I channel my life experiences into my books. I pay it forward and share how I learned to empower my mind, body, and soul. I studied Buddhist philosophy. I learned Transcendental and mindfulness meditation.

I devoured nearly every self-help book on the planet—and beyond. I went to healers and sought counseling.

I trained to be a hypnotherapist, counselor, and psychologist, and gained other therapeutic skills. I continue to pass on the knowledge I've learned to my clients and readers like you to help empower them to live your best lives.

Every day I fight for my dreams.

We all enter this life, and leave it, with different challenges. Different parents, siblings, life experiences. The pain of your past doesn't need to define you. If you are prepared to be honest and vulnerable and to do the work, you know what you need to do to empower your life and your work.

As Buddha once said, "It is better to conquer yourself than to win a thousand battles. Then the victory is yours. It cannot be taken from you, not by angels or by demons, heaven or hell."

If fear, wounds of the past, victim thinking, destructive health behaviors, or anything else detrimental to living your best life has a grip on you, prioritize breaking free.
Seeking help doesn't have to cost a fortune. You may heal your life with writing, work with a coach or therapist, or self-help your way to success.

When you seize the reins of control and take responsibility, you will empower your life—and your prosperity.

55

CULTIVATE HOPE

Leonardo da Vinci once wrote, "*One's thoughts turn towards hope.*"

The power of hope is grounded firmly in spiritual and religious practices but also in science. Like the ancient Greeks and Romans, da Vinci, and even 18th-century physicians, recognized the physiological effects of mind-power and hope on the body.

Successful medical outcomes, even when the intervention is a placebo, further evidence the impact of maintaining a positive expectation.

Dr. Joe Dispenza powerfully illustrates this fact in his fabulous book *You Are the Placebo: Making Your Mind Matter*.

If like me, and Joe Dispenza, you've manifested miracles in your own life by maintaining a positive expectation, you'll know the power of hope.

Thoughts *do* become things. Scientists Gregg Braden and Bruce Lipton, author of *The Biology of Belief*, have evidenced this.

But hope can only flourish when you believe that what you do can make a difference, that you recognize that you have choices and that your actions can create a future which differs from your present situation. Hope also requires faith.

When you empower your belief in your ability to gain some

control over your circumstances, you are no longer entirely at the mercy of forces outside yourself. You are back in the driving seat.

"Fearlessness is like a muscle. I know from my own life that the more I exercise it the more natural it becomes to not let my fears run me," says businesswoman, author, and founder of *The Huffington Post*, Arianna Huffington.

What you believe has a tremendous influence on the likelihood of success. Reframe your fears and buoy your dreams with hope. Not "I'm afraid of failing," but "I hope to succeed," or something similar.

Would you rather be a failure at something you love than a failure at something you hate? It's a question worth considering.

How could you cultivate more hope? If you felt the fear and did it anyway, what's the best that could happen?

56

ALLOW NO DOUBT

It's the messages you tell yourself that matter most, according to celebrity hypnotherapist and author Marisa Peer.

"Belief without talent will get you further than talent with no belief. If you have the two you will be unstoppable."

You may not be aware of your own self-limiting thoughts, beliefs, and patterns, or the negative, confining impact of others' beliefs about you.

Perhaps you've defined your life according to what others think you are capable of or believe you should settle for.

To slay the doubt demons and get at some of the core beliefs standing between you and the success you desire, you must interview your own beliefs.

Ask yourself the following questions:

"Where's your evidence for that?" ("that" being whatever you fear or hold to be true)

"What's the worst that could happen? How bad would that really be?"

"How can you increase the likelihood of success?"

"What tells you that you could follow your dreams?" (a nice shift from focusing on the problem is to look for solutions instead).

"What have you tried recently that worked? What are you doing now that works?"

"Who do you know that is a prosperous author? What could you learn from them?"

"How does your (supportive other) know you can do this? What difference will it make to them when you are happier, prosperous and more successful?"

AFFIRM WHAT YOU Want to be True

Your doubts are demons—they will destroy your dreams if you surrender without a fight.

Attitude is everything. Be a guard for your words, thoughts, and feelings. Always affirm what you want to be true and don't let self-doubt be the thing that deflates you.

Winners are too busy to be sad, too positive to be doubtful, too optimistic to be fearful, too focused on success and too determined to be defeated.

Be your biggest fan. Back yourself 100 percent. We all have doubts, but it's amazing how your doubts will disappear once you're doing the things you love.

Are you your biggest fan or worst enemy? How can you stay positive, confident, and optimistic?

Be your own CBT (Cognitive Behavioral Therapy) counselor, continually challenge unhelpful or irrational beliefs, and empower your beliefs with feeling-based affirmations.

DIVE DEEPER...

You'll find other helpful strategies to boost your beliefs in my book, *Boost Your Self-Esteem and Confidence: Six Easy Steps to Increase Self-Confidence, Self-esteem, Self-Value and Love Yourself More*.

I've also included a helpful section in my book, *Mid-Life Career Rescue: What Makes You Happy.* In this book, I share my experience following reading The Biology of Belief: Unleashing the Power of Consciousness, Matter & Miracles, by Dr. Bruce Lipton.

THE CHAPTERS which follow will help keep doubt low and confidence high.

57

FIGHT FOR YOUR DREAMS

Remember your dreams and fight for them. You must know what you want from life. There is just one thing that makes dreams become impossible: the fear of failure.

~ Paulo Coelho, author

Novelist Steven Pressfield called it as it is when he titled his non-fiction book *The War of Art*.

It's war out there with many opponents—time, temptation, distraction, economic uncertainty, family, work demands, and more.

Very often you may find that you are your own worst enemy and are either consciously or unconsciously sabotaging your success.

As Jessie Burton, a successful novelist who suffers from anxiety once said, "If you really want to see your work to completion you have to desire it more than you believe. You have to fight it, fight yourself. It's not easy."

Paulo Coehlo and other successful artists agree. "Remember your dreams and fight for them. You must know what you want from life.

There is just one thing that makes dreams become impossible: the fear of failure."

To help overcome some of the many things impeding your dreams, you must strive to acquire the following mindsets:

1.) **A willingness to persevere**. Many authors' first novels, and their subsequent ones, even when they were at the height of their fame, were rejected.

"Perseverance is absolutely essential, not just to produce all those words, but to survive rejection and criticism," J.K. Rowling once wrote.

2.) **An ability to handle criticism—even laugh at it**. At a writer's conference I attended several years ago, Micheal Cunningham, the Pulitzer Prize-winning author of *The Hours*, was told by a man, "I loved your first book but I hate this one. I really think you've lost it."

I was shocked and the audience was aghast. After taking a moment to compose himself, Michael, who is openly gay, smiled and said, "I'm sorry if we have to break up over this honey. I write the books I want to read. If you like it great. If not, that's fine too."

The audience laughed and Michael's light-hearted and humorous response only added to his appeal.

3.) **An ability to fear less.** Many authors are self-critical about their abilities. Some feel anxiety, others despondency. Elizabeth Gilbert, author of *Eat, Pray, Love*, once shared how she feared she would never write another #1 bestselling book. But she showed up and wrote more books any way.

She's used this same courage to announce that she is now in a same-sex relationship with a woman who was diagnosed with cancer.

"Death—or the prospect of death—has a way of clearing away everything that is not real," she said. "In that space of stark and utter realness, I was faced with this truth: I do not merely love Rayya; I am in love with Rayya. And I have no more time for denying that truth."

In the end, what matters is being true to yourself and cherishing the dreams which feel most real.

"I stopped pretending to myself that I was anything other than what I was, and began to direct all my energy into finishing the only work that mattered to me," J.K. Rowling once said.

How skillfully are you fighting for your dream of becoming a prosperous author?

OTHER THAN FINISHING and applying the strategies in this book, what additional tools, support, or weapons could help you fight through the blocks and win your inner creative battles?

How CAN you stay true to your vision and commit to finishing the work that really matters?

58

FINANCIAL RESCUE

Many people dream of being an artist, writing a book or making a living from their passion but say that lack of spare cash is holding them back. They often prevent themselves from choosing what they want to do because they fear there won't be the necessary money or support to allow it.

But money doesn't have to be an obstacle to seeking more fulfilling work, or finding a way to stress less.

Financing a career change, despite all the obstacles in your way, involves a conscious commitment to move forward and a willingness to think laterally and pragmatically about a range of financial options.

There are many different ways to finance a career change, including: consolidating debt, future-gazing and demand creation, career combo-ing, seeking investors, using equity, reducing outgoings, generating extra cash flow, and applying for funding.

The discipline needed to reprioritize your finances will be easier, and the sacrifices more bearable, if you allow your desire to drive you. Let's take a closer look at some of the possible financing options:

Rewrite your goals. List all the benefits making a change will bring. These may include better health, more money in the longer term, or improved relationships with loved ones.

Assess your current situation. Get an accurate picture of all your outgoings and expenses. Consolidate debt. Seek financial advice if necessary.

Get a reality check on your future plans. Is there a current or future demand for your writing? Could you create one? What is the true cost of making a change? Isolate costs against benefits: cash in against cash out. How much money do you really need to spend and create?

Earn more. Think laterally to create cash flow. A job doesn't have to be a full-time thing. Can you finance your career by doing a career-combo, working in a variety of different ways, or for several employers? Many people work at several jobs to earn extra cash.

Generate extra cash flow by increasing the money you earn. Some possible strategies include: negotiating a pay rise in your current position; taking on a new higher-paying role; or turning a hobby into cash flow.

New Zealand based and *USA Today* bestselling historical romance author Bronwen Evans, for example, took on a high-paying, high-pressure, one-year communications contract to allow her to take a year off so she could pursue her dream of becoming a full-time novelist.

Seek investors. Use other people's money to create the momentum you need. Remember there's good borrowing—borrowing to increase wealth, and bad borrowing—borrowing so you can consume more. Most people spend all their spare income on non-asset-producing consumption.

Banks, family members, and friends are all possible sources of investment income. Sam Morgan, who established the on-line trading company TradeMe, convinced his dad to back him and earned millions of dollars in return. You may not pay back millions, but if your idea is sound, your investors can sleep at night knowing they will be repaid.

Utilize equity. Burt Munro, whose story was made famous in the movie *The World's Fastest Indian*, mortgaged his home. Could you use the equity in your own home to finance your career? If you don't want to re-mortgage, you could try asking for a mortgage holiday. Many banks allow 2–3 months of no mortgage payments.

As fashion designer Calvin Klein once said, "I took the risk of putting my money on the line for the company." Are you prepared to do the same thing?

Share the load. Who else has a stake in your success? Perhaps they may be able to inject more cash into your joint cash flow or pitch in and share the family load.

New Zealand romance author Leanna Morgan asked her husband to take on the day-to-day family commitments so she could focus on her writing.

Today, she's a *USA Today* bestselling author who sells up to 300 books a day and has legions of fans in America. She's also the CEO of her own publishing company.

In just two years, Morgan has gone from an unknown writer to one who earns over $200,000 a year, allowing the mother-of-two to give up her job as a Libraries and Arts Manager to concentrate on her writing.

She recently shared with me that her goal is to make a million dollars, and more, from her writing.

"If anyone had told me two years ago that I'd be able to resign from a job I loved to become a full-time writer and publisher, I would have smiled and thought they were slightly crazy. But believe it or not, that's what happened," she told journalist Anna Kenna.

"Her success has not been without sacrifice, including little sleep and less time with husband Tim and her two children, aged 12 and 17," Kenna writes in her article.

"'I'd be up at 5.30am, getting in a few hours of writing before work, and writing in the evening when everybody else was asleep.'"

So she could devote herself to writing, Leanna's husband Tim shared more of their responsibilities.

"'Tim took over running the house and organizing our children,'" Morgan says. "'He did it to support me, but also because he could see the potential benefits of my success for the whole family.'"

Sharing the load, hard work, and commitment have yielded success beyond her and her family's dreams.

"'It's taken away the financial stress, allowed us to take a nice holiday and to look forward to a future we never considered possible,'" she says.

Find out more about Leanna Morgan at www.leeannamorgan.com and read the rest of this article, including why it's a brilliant time to be an independent author, here: www.stuff.co.nz/entertainment/books/85799137/How-one-Kiwi-author-is-making-200-000-a-year-publishing-romance-novels-online.

Reduce outgoings. Review your current commitments and expenditure. Proactively look around to make sure you are getting the best deal possible on your insurance, mobile phone plans, mortgages, and other regular financial commitments. Take note of your savings and squirrel the extra money away for a rainy day.

John, a coaching client of mine, shopped around for a better deal on his household insurance and saved himself over $600 annually in premiums. He also negotiated an installment plan with creditors so that he could increase his credit debt repayments, saving over $5,400 in interest charges annually.

Get funded. Many people and organizations offer sponsorship and various forms of funding to help people pursue their dreams. Without the help of a grant from Creative New Zealand, author Lloyd Jones may never have written *Mr. Pip*—the same book for which he won the prestigious and lucrative Man Booker Prize. The book was later made into a film.

Check out crowdfunding as an option, as Heather Morris initially shared in the chapter "Knock the Bugger Off." Her attempts to finance her film script lead to a multi-national publishing deal.

Multiply your income streams. When "authorpreneur" Kevin Kruse made the move to self-employment, he decided to record his financial success, complete with the highs and lows, by publicly sharing his income reports on his blog. There's lots of inspiration for anyone about to embrace change here: http://authorjourneyto100k.com/income-report-december-2015-and-full-year/.

Like many business people, Kruse knew early on that having a variety of income streams would help him manage cash-flow.

"I went into this whole thing knowing that to make the money I wanted to make I would need to diversify my income. I knew I'd need to spend time speaking, creating online courses, and marketing."

It is a common and successful strategy used by many business people, especially those working creatively. Ruth Pretty, for example, is a chef, newspaper columnist, cookbook writer, wedding venue provider, caterer, and cooking school tutor. The common theme? Her pursuits all center around her passion for food.

Amongst other things, photographer Carla Coulson is a portrait photographer, magazine photojournalist, tutor, and travel photographer. At the time of writing, she has retrained as a life coach and now offers creativity coaching and wellness workshops.

Italian designer Giorgio Armani has a flourishing clothing empire, a swag of luxury hotels, a music production company, and an interior design business. And these are just a few of his multi-billion-dollar revenue lines.

I am a self-empowerment author, coach, holistic psychologist, romance writer, brand manager, and novelist of art-related historical fiction. I also write marketing materials (blogs, newsletters, website content, etc.) for small businesses, and train people to become certified life and career coaches.

As my writing income grows, I'm making a conscious decision to spend less time in some of these areas and more in others.

You may wish to focus on one income stream, but if this doesn't work for you, consider diversifying. This will help you ride any fluctuating financial currents.

Remind yourself that money is not a measure of your true worth. Clarify what's important to you. As business magnate Richard Branson said, "I don't work for money, that's too shallow a goal." Lucky for him, his passion for having fun has netted him millions—as it has for James Patterson and other prosperous authors.

Whatever path you choose, be sure to work with love. Sonia Choquette, author of *Your Heart's Desire*, echoes this view: "When you work with love you draw others to you. Embrace this truth. The reason for this is that love is the highest vibration on earth. When you work with love people feel it, are helped by it, and return to it. That's why love is the best marketing tool around. Because it is so attractive, it pulls right to you what you need."

THE MONEY or Your Life

His Holiness the Dalai Lama once said, "Choose a job that allows the opportunity for some creativity and for spending time with your family. Even if it means less pay—it is better to choose work that is less demanding, that gives you greater freedom, more time to be with your family and friends, engage in cultural activities or just play. I think that is best."

This really spoke to me and was one of the primary reasons I chose to scale back my successful international consultancy. Time is more valuable to me than money. I can always find ways to get more money, but it is impossible to find more than 24 hours in any one day.

Be careful what you chase. Is it more money, or a better quality of life? With planning, it just may be possible to do both, says Tim Ferris in his bestselling book *The 4-Hour Work Week*.

YOU MAY NOT HAVE the cash at the moment, and the economy may not be ideal, but that doesn't mean your mind can't be working on your ideas and creating the way to a better future. Look for opportunities in every climate. That's leverage.

How could you finance your writing career?

DIVE DEEPER...

FINANCIAL RESCUE: The Total Money Makeover: Create Wealth, Reduce Debt & Gain Freedom

You may not have the cash at the present moment, and the economy may not be ideal, but that doesn't mean your mind can't be working on your ideas and creating the way to a better future. My book *Financial Rescue* will show you how to reduce debt and create opportunities in every climate.

59

SORT IT

Sometimes life can feel like an obstacle race. Having things in your way will slow down your ability to bounce and can completely stop you in your tracks.

Things in your way could be things you have to do, but put off doing. For example, revamping your resume, having conversations that are a little uncomfortable, or paying bills.

If you don't sort them, not only will they prevent you from being able to bounce, but ongoing procrastination, denial and putting your head in the sand will leave you feeling despondent and flat.

Get things sorted without delay. Tackle the things you least want to do first—they are usually your biggest rocks. But the payoff and rewards for completing these tasks can be liberating.

Rather than have a to-do list you may decide to put in place a not to do list.

'What should we simplify?'" Tim Ferris writes in his bestselling book, *Tools of Titans*. "Adding elements to your business strategy is often expensive and time-consuming but removing things isn't."

Ferriss says, "I've since applied this 'What if I could only subtract ...?' to my life in many areas, and I sometimes rephrase it as 'What should I put on my not-to-do list?'"

Here are some of the things many successful people vow **not** to do, or do less of, to stress less and be more empowered:
- Procrastinating
- Working on tasks that are low value
- Doing small things first
- Surfing the internet incessantly
- Not paying bills on time
- Spending too long on Facebook and social media
- Getting involved in extra activities
- Relentless perfectionism
- Avoiding facing issues or seeking help

Decluttering is another simple, but effective way, to simplify your life. Your environment very often mirrors your inner world. Chaos leads to stress and exhaustion, ending in physical and emotional depletion.

When faced with overwhelm, sometimes the best place to start is somewhere simple.

Perhaps the sock drawer. Just how many mismatched socks is it possible to store? The windows, just how much brighter is your room once the grime has been removed? These, and other simple steps, will yield immediate results.

"There is a calm that can ascend when we're quietly busy with seemingly mundane tasks. Our minds are free to drift and muse, and in the spaciousness of busyness, new solutions to old problems have room to appear," says Melanie Spears, creator of *The Gratitude Diary*.

Declutter. Embrace the elemental art of simplicity. Remove things from your life that don't spark joy. Do the important things and ignore the trivial—it will make a real difference to your energy levels, your life and your career.

60

TAKE RESPONSIBILITY

Whatever is going on in your life you must take personal responsibility. You may not be able to change the circumstances, But changing yourself is something you can control.

It can take courage to take ownership of your health, happiness, and success. Taking responsibility can mean ending years of blaming others.

Taking responsibility is the ultimate of freedoms. The freedom to be yourself and to choose what happens to you. Coco Chanel once said that she didn't want to weigh more heavily on a man than a bird. She fought for her independence, and created an enduring fortune in the process.

But it's not just about the money. People who take complete responsibility for their lives often experience profound joy and the confidence and added security of knowing they are in the driving seat.

They are able to make wise choices because they know they have ultimate responsibility for those choices and can control how they react to setbacks.

If blaming others or making excuses plays repeatedly in your mind, you are shifting **responsibility** for your decisions and life to others. It's time for some tough and compassionate self-love.

- Eliminate blame, eliminate excuses.
- Commit to an excuse-free diet. Take one hundred percent responsibility for your actions, your thoughts, and your goals. Monitor and be a guard for your words, thoughts and actions.
- Spend time thinking about, and taking action towards your goals, dreams, and desires. Become audaciously inspired and empowered by your visions of success.
- Live every day as if what you do matters—because it does. Every choice you make; every action you take—matters. Your choices matter to you and to the life you live.
- Bounce higher—create your best life by taking back control.

61

ELIMINATE NEGATIVE EMOTIONS

Toxic emotions, including anxiety, depression, anger, and resentment, if left unresolved, are insidious thieves of energy and vitality.

Avoid Groundhog Day. Don't let people, things, or situations which trigger unhealed wounds or that spark irritability take you prisoner. Pinpoint the causes and look for solutions.

Resist the urge to play "victim." In the short term, it may seem like the easy option, but long term, this unresolved source of stress will create havoc on your mind, body, and soul.

Anger prepares your body to fight, and it does a lot of damage to your brain and body if you're in a situation where you sustain those stress chemicals. The Thymus gland begins to shrivel up and this can make you susceptible to internal organ ulceration.

Anger can even kill you. A new study in the journal *Social Science and Medicine* found that the angrier you are the most likely you are to have health problems and die early.

Furthermore, when you trigger the stress response by getting angry, it effectively disengages the thinking part of the brain, the cerebral cortex – which is fine if you need to launch into combat. Though it doesn't help if you need to choose the best response, to stop and muse on the merits of your chosen course of action.

There is incredibly wide-spread ignorance of how emotions actually work. People struggle with the idea that we can choose our emotions. It is impossible for anyone to make another person angry, sad, depressed, or happy—without their consent. There is always a point of choice, no matter how fleeting this decisive moment may seem.

Drowning in a sea of negativity or keeping baggage from the past will leave no room for happiness in the future.

Avoid choices which weaken your life energy: shame, guilt, confusion, fear, hatred, pride, hopelessness, and falsehood. Embrace those that lift you higher: truth, courage, acceptance, reason, love, beauty, joy, and peace.

If you're struggling to deal with negative emotions there's a wealth of help on hand. Self-help your way to success; talk to a supportive, wise friend, or seek advice from a counselor, psychologist, life coach, or other expert. Remember, "a problem shared is a problem solved."

Consider reading my *Millionaire Mindset* book. Even though it was written for authors, the strategies apply to anyone who wants to overcome negative emotions and develop more empowering beliefs.

62

CHANGE THE WAY YOU REACT

By change of reaction comes a change of circumstance, say many great spiritual masters and teachers. If you are distressed, or feeling anxious or in a low mood, taking back control can prove challenging. It is hard to feel energized and optimistic when you are overwhelmed, depleted, and despairing.

It's hard—but not impossible. Viktor Frankl, an Austrian psychiatrist who survived the horrors of Nazi death camps, believed that it's not the situation which defines and controls us, but our attitudes and reactions. The key to his survival, Frankl maintained, was searching for meaning in that which seems unfathomable.

Stressed or not, you can determine your reaction."Between stimulus and response there is a space. In that space is our power to choose our response. In our response lies our growth and our freedom, Frankl said.

Ensure success at becoming less stressed and more empowered by:

- Focusing on three good things you have done each day
- Praising yourself when you achieve a result
- Practicing radical acceptance of yourself, or the situation, if you feel stressed

- Find meaning and purpose in your experience.

In my book *Stress Less. Love Life More: How to Stop Worrying, Reduce Anxiety, Eliminate Negative Thinking and Find Happiness,* I shared strategies to help you transcend the biological stress reaction before it overpowers you. Listed below are two simple strategies:

Reinterpret the situation: e.g., change the meaning; instead of "they should do what I want," try, "I'm learning how to cope with other peoples' demands."

Modify or remove the stressor/s: e.g., assertive action; prioritize; work reasonable hours; quit a job you hate.

BOUNCE back from setbacks and proactively choose high-vibration responses. As David Hawkins writes in *Power vs. Force*, "Love is more powerful than hatred; truth sets you free; forgiveness liberates both sides; unconditional love heals; courage empowers; and the essence of Divinity/Reality is peace."

63

BOUNCE MEMORIES THAT SUCK

If you change your beliefs you will change your life. That's great to know—but how do you do that in way that lasts?

To better understand why some memories create disempowering beliefs that are hard to shift, let's take a wee wander around the brain.

Stressful or emotionally intense experiences stimulate hormones that activate parts of the brain associated with housing memories and emotions. The secretion of epinephrine (adrenaline) and cortisol stimulate the amygdala.

The amygdala in turn stimulates the hippocampus and the cerebral cortex, which are both important for memory storage. However, excessive or prolonged stress, with correspondingly prolonged cortisol, impairs memory.

This explains why people find it so difficult to forget traumatic and stressful events—often replaying them again and again in their minds. The emotional charge that the event held consolidates and strengthens the memory into long-term storage.

If the traumatic event is not processed and worked through, the emotional charge remains, locking it further in the cellular structure of the brain. Counseling or reprogramming using hypnosis are some of the many techniques that may be necessary to help you **change your view of the event**.

For example, one effective and powerful counseling technique used to assist people who are suffering from Post-Traumatic Stress Disorder is called "Rapid Eye Desensitization." It works by removing/altering the previous bio-chemical or structural change the trauma of the event created.

Whilst counseling and reframing techniques in general can help you to gain a new perspective, "Rapid Eye Desensitization" weakens the emotional charge.

SHIFTING **Self-Limiting Beliefs**

Traumatic memories leave a residue of unhelpful beliefs; yet so often, we aren't even aware of what our self-limiting beliefs are. If your unhelpful thoughts are ingrained, or you keep sabotaging your own success, seeking help from a qualified practitioner with expertise in reprogramming stubborn, disempowering beliefs may be a game-changer.

A wonderful counselor with whom I trained to be a Worklife Solutions Certified Life Coach recommended the book *The Biology of Belief: Unleashing the Power of Consciousness, Matter & Miracles*, by Bruce Lipton.

Lipton is an American developmental biologist best known for promoting the idea that genes and DNA can be manipulated by a person's beliefs.

In his book, he shares how he experienced a paradigm shift while at a conference. Back then, Lipton, like so many of us, didn't fully realize the crucial role the subconscious mind plays in the change process.

"Instead, I relied mostly on trying to power through negative behavior, using positive thinking and willpower. I knew, though, that I had had only limited success in making personal changes in my own life.

"I also knew that when I offered this solution, the energy in the room dropped like a lead balloon. It seems my sophisticated audiences had already tried willpower and positive thinking with limited success."

Fate intervened for Lipton, as it did for me when I was guided to his book. So often life whispers to us, but we fail to tune in. In Lipton's case, the messenger he needed to hear was sitting right next to him; psychotherapist Rob Williams, the creator of the self-help tool PSYCH-K, was presenting at the same conference.

"Rob's opening remarks quickly had the entire audience on the edge of our seats. In his introduction, Rob stated that PSYCH-K can change long-standing, limiting beliefs in a matter of minutes," Lipton wrote.

In his book *The Biology of Belief*, Lipton shares how, in less than 10 minutes, a woman paralyzed by her fear of public speaking transformed into a confident, excited, and visibly relaxed person up on the stage. The transformation Lipton witnessed was so astounding, he has since used PYSCH-K in his own life.

"PSYCH-K has helped me undo my self-limiting beliefs, including one about not being able to finish my book," Lipton wrote at the end of his book.

That struck a chord with me. I felt a trill of excitement. Not a thrill, but a trill—a song deep in my heart. Lipton was like the Pied Piper and I was happy to follow. At the time, I had so many unfinished books and had published nothing.

A month after working with a PSYCH-K trained practitioner, I finished the first two books in my *Mid-Life Career Rescue* series. Soon after, I released my third, *Midlife Career Rescue: Employ Yourself*, followed quickly by a fourth book, *How to Find Your Passion and Purpose*.

At the time of writing, I have also published three romance books under my pen name, Mollie Mathews.

Now, you're reading my sixteenth book—all completed within the last two years. All because, despite feeling skeptical (and a little vulnerable), I sought help to reprogram my mindset.

If traumatic memories or unhelpful beliefs are ingrained, or you keep sabotaging your own success, seeking help from a qualified practitioner with expertise in reprogramming stubborn, disempowering beliefs may be a game-changer.

You may not need to see a therapist to move beyond self-limiting beliefs; but if you do, go and get help. There's magic in that.

You can also learn from some of the most powerful, effective, and simple techniques used by practitioners working in the realm of positive psychology and mind reprogramming. This includes hypnosis—something you'll discover in the next chapter.

64

HAPPY HYPNOSIS

UK based hypnotherapist Marissa Peer says that there are only three things you need to know about your mind: it likes what is familiar, it responds to the pictures in your head, and it gravitates to what you desire.

To get the tremendous power of your unconscious mind behind your goals, you will need to program it for success. A simple and exceedingly effective way to do this is through hypnosis.

"Emotional problems work much more on the 'feeling level' than the 'thinking level' which is why just trying to think differently is so hard," say the UK-based hypnotherapists at Uncommon Knowledge.

"We use hypnosis to help you feel different quickly which then makes you think differently about a situation."

You can access hypnosis sessions from the comfort of your home via instant download. There's an endless array of scripts on offer to help you overcome self-doubt, increase confidence, reduce anxiety, overcome addictions and much more.

But a word of caution first—the Internet is awash with websites which offer hypnosis products and services that have not been created by experienced and qualified professionals. Some of these programs are of limited or no use, while others may do more harm than good.

"Hypnosis is the epitome of mind-body medicine. It can enable the mind to tell the body how to react and modify the messages that the body sends to the mind," reported the *New York Times* in a recent article.

Harness the power of your mind to put weight into your dreams, and to help you remove obstacles to your success. Experiment with this powerful technique and reprogram your subconscious mind for success.

Don't forget about the transformational power of self-hypnosis, affirmations and the self-soothing strategies I shared previously. Kind, encouraging, and sometimes stroppy self-talk can really help you bounce. Talk yourself up and enjoy a natural high.

65

PATIENT PERSEVERANCE

The best thing I can tell you? It's two words. Patient persistence.

Knowing when to quit is one thing; knowing when to persevere another. Whether it's the weight of obstacles you face, the setbacks and the disappointments, the successes others seem to achieve more speedily, or the critical feedback from others who are impatient to see more evidence that you'll make it—never give up. Never, never, never give up.

Many people's most enduring successes took years and years to achieve. Nora Roberts is probably the most successful romance novelist on the planet. Thirty-four of her titles are sold every minute and she earns an estimated $US60 million a year! But her success didn't happen in 6 months, a year, or even three.

She started writing back in the 1980's for Mills and Boon and then morphed into mainstream romance fiction—and other genres. So, I really shouldn't be discouraged when the three romance novels I published this year haven't filled my coffers with gold. Looking back, I also shouldn't have been discouraged by the feedback that I received early in my career that "my characters were dysfunctional." Instead of targeting Mills and Boon, the reviewer suggested that my romances seemed better suited to mainstream women's fiction—a path Roberts also pursued.

Along with Roberts' commitment to write characters she can personally identify with, it is her work ethic and her prolific output that really defines her. "Whatever I'm doing, I get very guilty if I don't put a good day's work in. I'm not one for making excuses. I had this Catholic upbringing. I was taught to finish what you start."

A prodigious work ethic, cultivated talent, commitment to finishing what she starts, over four different pen names, writing in a variety of genres, perseverance, and persistence are amongst the many things which have made her one of the world's most prosperous authors.

Award-winning, perennial bestselling author Jodi Picoult is the author of over twenty books, the last five of which debuted at No. 1 on the *New York Times* bestseller list. Her books have been translated into thirty-four languages, and four have been made into television movies, while another, *My Sister's Keeper*, was made into a film starring Cameron Diaz.

"I had over 100 rejection letters from agents. Finally, one woman who had never represented anyone in her life said she thought she could take me on. I jumped at the chance. She sold my first novel in three months," says Picoult.

Both authors, and others like them, wouldn't be where they are now if it weren't for their grit, persistence, and patient perseverance.

When you think of patience, perseverance, tenacity, and success, who comes to mind?

WHO OR WHAT can help you to manifest more persistence? How can you keep your mind on your vision, your body moving towards your dreams, your heart warmed by the joy you will feel when you finally achieve success?

66

KNOCK THE BUGGER OFF

Giving up on telling this story was never an option for me.

~ Heather Morris, author

I first met Heather Morris, the author of *The Tattooist of Auschwitz* (to be released in 2018) when she came to the Bay of Islands in New Zealand from her home in Melbourne.

Her novel is based on the true story of Slovakian Jew Lale Sokolov, who was forced to tattoo the numbers on his fellow victims' arms that would mark them for survival.

Sokolov used the infinitesimal freedom of movement that his position gave him to exchange jewels and money taken from murdered Jews for food to keep others alive.

"My book is the true story of the girl he fell in love with when he held her hand and tattooed a number on her left arm, and how they survived for two and a half years in that Dante-esque circle of hell, got separated, found each other, married, and lived very happily for over 50 years," Heather told me.

I invited Heather to share her story and she generously emailed me the following:

> I met Lale Sokolov in December 2003. I was 50-years old and had been dabbling in learning and writing screenplays; he was 87-years-old and his wife, Gita, had died two months earlier.
>
> A friend of a friend of their son, Gary, asked me to meet Lale to hear the secret he'd kept for over fifty years and which he wanted to tell someone before he 'hurried up and joined his beloved Gita.'
>
> Over the next three years, our friendship grew as, slowly, his story was revealed to me piecemeal, often told at bullet pace with limited coherency and with no flow or connection to the many, many stories he told.
>
> It didn't matter. I fell under his spell.
>
> Was it the delightful Eastern European accent? Was it the charm this old rascal had lived his life dispensing? Or, was it the twisted, convoluted story I was starting to make sense of—the significance and importance of which was beginning to dawn on me.
>
> It was all of these things and more. I was spending time with 'living history' and was being given a story to tell for which I am honored and privileged to have been entrusted with.
>
> Fast forward to 2017—14 years after my fateful meeting with Lale Sokolov. It took me two years to get the story I would eventually write into a screenplay. He got to read it and loved it.
>
> I sat with him and held his hand and said goodbye to him the night he died. At that time, I vowed to never stop trying to tell his story.
>
> A film production company optioned the script from me for three years, then another two years, but failed to 'get it up'.
>
> I took the option back and, after a rewrite, started entering it in screenplay competitions around the world. It did well, and was often a finalist and won the International Independent Film Award in 2016.
>
> I was receiving comments from film executives that the story 'not only should be told, but must be told;' that it was 'Oscar bait'. But still no-one came forward to talk production.
>
> Then a light-bulb moment came when I decided to write it as a

novel, something I had no experience with and had never written or studied as a writing medium.

On the advice of one of my sons to help with 'free promotion,' I did a Kickstarter campaign to raise funds to self-publish. From this campaign, a local publishing company in Melbourne approached me and signed me up.

I attempted to write while working full-time in a large Melbourne hospital and being the accommodating grandmother to my son and his wife, my daughter and her husband and their three little ones.

I was getting no-where.

I'm lucky to have family living in San Diego, California, who have a holiday house on the top of Big Bear Mountain. In the middle of their winter, in six feet of snow, I squirreled myself away for four weeks and as Sir Edmund Hilary once said, 'knocked the bugger off.'

The parent company of my publisher came to Melbourne in February and heard about my story. They have now taken over the publishing, sold foreign language rights to 13 countries, and done a deal with Harper Collins in the U.S. to publish there.

And the screenplay? Stay tuned—some heavy hitters in Hollywood are vying for it.

I am now 64 years old and about to embark on a journey beyond my wildest dreams as I travel promoting the book and hopefully, in two or three years' time, a film.

Giving up on telling this story was never an option for me. Yes, months went by when I did nothing to further it as life got in the way. I told myself it was *The Tattooist*'s time, I had to hang in there, seek out avenues to have the story heard and eventually one paid off.

I don't kid myself that I'm a great writer. I am privileged to have been given a great story to tell and I hope Lale and Gita would be proud of the job I've done telling their story. I have received the ultimate validation of my attempt from their son who doesn't want a word changed.

A lot of very talented people/editors both in Melbourne and London will produce a book which I am honored to have my name on.

My family keep telling me they wouldn't be doing that if I hadn't written it in the first place.

I have two quotes on the wall near my desk, the one mentioned above by Sir Edmund and one from one of my favorite screenwriters, William Goldman, who references the children's book *The Little Engine That Could*.

'Just get the @#%&% engine over the mountain.'"

Heather's story is a powerful reminder not to give up on your dreams. Tenacity, perseverance, patience, and the ability to adapt are big factors in her success—and many other attributes as well, including talent!

She began with a film script and then taught herself how to turn a script into a novel. She also taught herself to fund her dreams via the Internet—and then opportunity came knocking. But, importantly, success came because she put her work out there.

It's a reminder to us all that you grow into your dreams, and a commitment to continual learning is essential. As is hanging onto a success mindset.

As Heather said, giving up on telling this story was never an option for her. Heather also proves what Napoleon Hill so famously wrote in his classic book *Think and Grow Rich*—most people don't achieve their success until their sixties and beyond.

Winners never quit and quitters never win.

67

PRAYER THERAPY

Harness the energies of love and boost your ability to bounce and tenacity to succeed with the sacred daily ritual of prayer.

If prayer is something you are unfamiliar with or hold negative associations about, don't be deterred. Whatever your experience or belief system, prayer is simply a form of spiritual communion. It's a very simple and potent tool used successfully by many resilient people.

Many people have lost their union with God because of the hypocritical dogma which has polluted many faith systems. However, prayer comes in many shapes, colors, and textures.

Many prosperous creatives and successful business people, including Coco Chanel, Julia Cameron, Wayne Dyer and Louise Hay, refer to prayer in several forms, including describing it as the voice of God, intuition, higher self, inner goddess, or their Sacred Divine.

In her book *Illuminata: A Return to Prayer*, Marianne Williamson speaks of prayer as a way of "focusing our eyes," dramatically transforming our orientation, releasing us "from the snares of lower energies," and aligning "our internal energies with truth."

As the author of *The Alchemist*, Paulo Coelho, shares on the back jacket of his book, *The Spy*, "In searching for his own place in the world, he has discovered answers for the challenges that everybody faces. He believes that within ourselves, we have the necessary strength to find our destiny."

Prayer, or invoking a higher power, is revered by many for its power to help them reclaim their strength, find their inner power and overcome tragedy.

In their book *The Energies of Love*, intuitive healer Donna Eden and psychiatrist David Feinstein refer to the action of prayer as inviting an inspiring invocation.

Dictionary.com refers to an invocation as the "act of invoking or calling upon a deity, spirit, etc., for aid, protection, inspiration, or the like." The website also defines invocation as "an entreaty for aid and guidance from a Muse."

Saying a simple prayer "alerts your sensibilities to dimensions that your senses do not perceive," say Eden and Feinstein.

In their book, they share how they are not consistent with their use of invocations, but use them most when they are about to embark on anything creative.

"Dozens of mini-prayers have infused the writing of this book, sometimes asking for wisdom, clarity, focus, and humor; other times asking that you, dear reader, receive guidance that gives your relationship greater ease, depth, healing, and joy."

Below are a few examples of their collective and individual invocations:

> We ask that we touch people deeply and in ways that enhance their spirits, well-being, and mastery of their energies.
>
> I ask this day for opportunities to love, to flourish, and to heal that which thirsts for healing.
>
> I ask for support so that which is purest within me can shine through me.

Acting on the recommendation in their book to create my own invocation by referring to the writings of Rumi, one of my favorite poetic mystics, I wrote the below invocation from which I draw sustenance and purpose (my adaption appears in parentheses):

> I have one small drop of knowing in my soul. (Fill my heart with wisdom and) let it dissolve in your ocean (spreading healing waves of comfort, hope, and joy to all those who bathe in the waters of our words).

Scientific (4-step) prayer therapy is another form of invoking guidance and "the only real answer to the great deception," writes Joseph Murphy (PhD.) in his excellent book, *The Miracle of Mind Dynamics*. "Let the light of God shine in your mind, and you will neutralize the harmful effects of the negatives implanted in your subconscious mind."

The four steps Murphy suggests are:

- Recognition of the healing presence of Infinite Intelligence
- Complete acceptance of the One Power
- Affirmation of the Truth
- Rejoice and give thanks for the answer

"Faith is action in love," Mother Theresa once said. Whatever mode of prayer or invocation you use, read them slowly and deliberately and notice how the energies in your mind, body and soul shift.

The indicator of God's presence in you is the presence of peace, harmony, abundance, and joy.

Take the time to stop and pray from your heart. The words that you use aren't as important compared to the strength of your desire to connect with The Divine.

Be open to a response appearing which is different from your expectations—and know that your prayers are heard and answered.

68

GOOD VIBRATIONS

My daughter Hannah Joy is contributing this chapter about the power of music to help you bounce. Hannah is a gifted writer with an AMAZING voice, and an instinctive feel for music. Before she could walk or talk she would jive along to her favorite songs—one of which was Mustang Sally from the movie *The Commitments*. Here's what she wrote:

> There are so many ways that music can help you and heal you. It's the reason people train to become music therapists. But you don't need to have a degree to benefit from good vibrations.
>
> As a young girl I would spend countless hours dancing around my room to my iPod pretending I was at the Video Music Awards or the Grammys. Music helped me to escape my reality, but at the same time I was able to work with the Law of Attraction and manifest better things.
>
> I spent countless hours pretending I was on a film set, singing songs. When I was 25-years-old I manifested the opportunity of a life-time—to appear in a feature length musical film. It was recorded

in Peter Jackson's studio in Miramar, Wellington, and involved the New Zealand Symphony Orchestra. I was so excited!

Pythagoras was the first known person to use Music Therapy to help people with mental afflictions. This practice has been used to overcome adversity for thousands of years.

We first begin to respond to music in the womb. In the last trimester as babies we are able to hear musical sound.

We develop our innate capacity to move to a beat and to feel a beat. The rhythm of our mother's heartbeat is the first beat we respond to as fetuses.

Tones and sounds affect our psychology. Listening to peaceful music can help you to sleep just as upbeat music can lift your mood. If I ever feeling sad I put on a happy song.

Music can be used for comfort. Music can be used to empower the passage of sadness. Music can induce a relaxation response—especially some classical music.

It's not just the melodies though, it's also the lyrics and the stories people tell with their words. For me, the lyrics in Taylor Swift's 1989 album helped me to overcome a terrible breakup.

Her vulnerability and the rawness of her lyrics were so uplifting for me. It helped me feel less alone in my experience to know that she had felt the same confusions and frustrations too. This was the album where she released the song "Shake it Off."

Shaking it off is a brilliant way to bounce back. Sometimes we get far too bogged down in reality and we simply need to return to our inner child and have some fun. Plug in those headphones, put a happy playlist on Spotify and dance around the house.

Crystal bowls are one of the most powerful musical healers. These bowls send sound vibrations through the room that have healing energies that vibrate through our bodies. Its actually physics, so there is science behind this. Just like Shaman healers use drums for their healing purposes. Sound healing has been used around the globe for centuries.

The didgeridoo is considered one of the world's oldest musical instruments. This instrument is fast becoming accepted as a form of treatment for sleep apnea. This instrument of the indigenous Australians facilitates meditation, states of harmony and balance—among other bouncy things!

Sound healing, whether it's from your favorite song, they rhythmic wash of waves on the seashore, or an ancient musical instrument is one of the cheapest and easiest ways to access healing and to recover when life's hurdles knock us down.

If you need some help bouncing go search for your favorite sound.

MUSIC MAKES you feel less isolated and things like Spotify make it easy to choose the mood, and avoid repetitive sounds tracks.

69

GOOD ENOUGH

Perfectionism will keep you poor, " says photographer Carla Coulson.

No story, no painting, no work of art is ever "finished." There's always something to change, to add, to remove. Good art pulsates with living energy—just like we do. There's always room for growth.

I know writers who have been "polishing" the same novel for tens of years. I was once one of them.

The challenge is knowing when to let go and release your baby into the world.

The truth is if you overwork your creative project you can ruin its vibrancy, its essence, the energy that inspired you to create it in the first place. You run the risk of becoming paralyzed by perfection, becoming sick of your creation, and losing your passion.

Someone once said, "It's like an itch you don't have to scratch, because every time you read your story, you'll always find something that needs to be changed. And if you feel like your story is perfect, just take a few weeks' break, then read it again. Suddenly, it won't feel as good as you previously thought."

Adopt a new mantra—the good enough mantra. Remind yourself "it's good enough." Know that, especially in this modern era of publishing, you can always go back to it later. But for now, you have to get things done, and you have to release them to the world.

Just like blowing bubbles, some will fly just for a few seconds, others will never get off the ground, while others will soar eternally towards the sky.

But working on the same writing project for much longer than is healthy is just as bad as starting a hundred different things and never finishing any of them.

I used to be afraid to let go of my work. I was terrified of what people might think of my books; I was worried they weren't good enough.

I still care, but I care less. I think it was Leonardo da Vinci who said that those who don't doubt their ability will never reach their heights.

We all want to be better, but I know from experience that advancement is made only by moving forward.

If people like the books I write, great. If they don't, then I know that I have done the best I can do right now, and I welcome their constructive feedback to help me improve.

You only get better at creating by creating a lot, not by editing the same project for two decades.

Done is better than striving for the impossible—perfection. Avoid over-working your writing projects—let your work go out into the world knowing it is as good as it can be right now.

COMMIT TO CONTINUAL IMPROVEMENT—IN your new work and the books that follow.

70

PASSION JOURNAL TIPS

It's staggeringly, and dishearteningly, true that many people don't know what they are passionate about. Some research suggests that only 10% of people are living and working with passion. Hence my passion for passion— to bring about positive change in the world. Creating a passion journal is one simple but powerful technique to help achieve this.

The purpose of the Passion Journal is to encourage you to create and stay focused on your preferred future and goals and to build greater awareness of your own unique passion criteria.

The Passion Journal taps into the principles of The Law of Attraction and Law of Intention to help you manifest your dreams. It acts as a central, easily retrievable place to collect and store sources of inspiration, insights, and clues related to your passion, career goals, and preferred future. It is also a motivational tool to be updated regularly and looked at frequently—ideally daily.

According to mind-mapping and creativity expert Tony Buzan, we think in images not words. Surround yourself with images that symbolize or reflect the things you want to create. Allow these images to inspire and excite you. Add a dose of color and engage all your senses.

Keeping a journal gives you a sense of your own story. In a sense you create a script for your own life as you go along.

I was clearing out some of my old journals the other day when I came across something I had written back in 2000. "I will live in a house that is elevated with lots of sunshine, and which is surrounded by trees. It will be elegant and streamlined, with simplicity at its core and feng-shuied to make sure it is the best it can be."

What amazed me was not what I had written but the astonishing realization that seven years later I was living in the house I had created first in my imagination.

I achieved the same result when I began manifesting moving to a lifestyle property. I now live on a gorgeous 10-acre property overlooking the beautiful Bay of Islands.

I have done the same thing in my career. Gathering images of the ingredients of career satisfaction, helped me see my way to career success and to direct my job creation activities much more efficiently.

I even manifested my dream man! Now, that's powerful creativity!

It's also one of the principals of the Law of Attraction made infamous by the DVD *The Secret*. But guess what? There is no secret! What there is instead is a lack of conscious awareness about how to tap into the law of attraction to make your dreams and goals a reality.

CREATING YOUR PASSION JOURNAL

Choosing the right book and designing your cover

To be effective choose a journal no smaller than A4 with blank pages—to free up your linear brain it's important there are no lines.

THE COVER of your journal is very important. Every time you look at it, it will reinforce your key theme/s. Choose a color or image for the front cover which symbolizes what you want to experience, or how you want to feel about your future. These colors and images will reinforce optimism and purpose on a subconscious level and help you maintain your focus.

If you can't find a journal with the ideal cover don't let this stop you. Create one. Every year I go to my local art store and choose a blank A4 visual diary with a hard white cover. I then create my theme.

One year I drew a simple red circle – symbolizing (for me) spirituality, the Divine Feminine, going with the flow and many other themes important to me that year.

In 2014, I created the cover of my passion journal by gluing a photo of a painting I purchased by one of my favorite artists, Max Gimblett, who is also a Zen Buddhist monk.

I included a quote, and added the words: "The art spirit." This reinforced my key theme of focusing on my creativity that year. The color of the painting was important to me, too, violet and green, symbolizing spirituality, growth, and renewal.

Other clients have chosen a single image or a color such as yellow (to boost optimism). Again, there is no right way— only the way that speaks to who you are and who you choose to be.

Unleash your creativity

Adding lots of images and color is an important part of manifesting your desires. Gather anything that matches or provides clues to your passion.

These may be clippings from magazines, words and phrases that affirm what you want, pictures of people who are doing the sort of work you want to do, or who inspire you in any way.

Add any other inspirational information and imagery that affirms and reinforces your intentions. Get your felt tip pens out, a glue stick and scissors and unchain your inner child.

You may also want to paste logos of companies you want to work for—or create your own logo if you dream of self-employment.

Add job advertisements and position descriptions that excite you.

If more romance is what you're after, or better health and worklife balance—you know what to do!

. . .

You'll find more tips to help you create a passion journal and manifest your dreams and goals easily in my book, *The Passion-Driven Business Planning Journal: The Effortless Path to Manifesting Your Business and Career Goals. Available from your favorite online bookstore.*

71

FOLLOW YOUR PASSION AND PURPOSE TO PROSPERITY ONLINE COACHING PROGRAM

Easily discover your passion and purpose, overcome barriers to success, and create a job or business you love with my self-paced online course.

Gain unlimited lifetime access to this course, for as long as you like— across any and all devices you own. Be supported with practical, inspirational, easy to access strategies to achieve your dreams.

Quit just existing and start really living! Start this course now to achieve outstanding personal and professional results with absolute certainty and excitement. **Click here to enroll— https://the-coaching-lab.teachable.com/p/follow-your-passion-and-purpose-to-prosperity**

IN *FOLLOW YOUR Passion and Purpose to Prosperity:* you'll learn:

- Why successful people follow their passion, not their pension
- How to identify your REAL priorities
- How working with passion can cure many modern-day ills—stress, depression, anxiety, overwhelm and boredom

- How to be happy and successful
- How to boost your self-esteem and super-charge the confidence needed to make an inspired change
- How to discover your signature gifts and talents and confirm your work-related strengths
- How to change jobs and find a career you will enjoy, including self-employment
- How identifying your PPT will increase profit, peace and prosperity
- How to overcome obstacles to your success

ENROL TODAY and receive these bonus gifts—FREE copies from a selection of my Amazon best-selling books:

Mid-Life Career Rescue (Employ Yourself): How to Confidently Leave a Job You Hate, and Start Living a Life You Love, Before It's Too Late

FIND YOUR PASSION AND PURPOSE: Four Easy Steps to Discover A Job You Want And Live the Life You Love

BOOST YOUR SELF-ESTEEM: Six Easy Steps to Increase Self-Confidence, Self-esteem, Self-Value and Love Yourself More

STRESS LESS. Love Life More: How to Stop Worrying, Reduce Anxiety, Eliminate Negative Thinking and Find Happiness

The Little Princess

**CLICK HERE to enroll and grab this TIME LIMITED OFFER—
https://the-coaching-lab.teachable.com/p/follow-your-passion-and-purpose-to-prosperity**

CONCLUSION

GRAB YOUR FREE GIFT!

The Passion Journal: The Effortless Path to Manifesting Your Love, Life, and Career Goals

Thank you for your interest in my new book.
To show my appreciation, I'm excited to be giving you another book for FREE!

Download the free *Passion Journal Workbook* here>>https://dl.bookfunnel.com/aepj97k2n1

I hope you enjoy it—it's dedicated to helping you live and work with passion, resilience and joy.

You'll also be subscribed to my newsletter and receive free giveaways, insights into my writing life, new release advance alerts and inspirational tips to help you live and work with passion, joy, and prosperity. Opt out at anytime.

SUMMARY OF HOLISTIC STRATEGIES

Throughout this book you've discovered ways to overcome find happiness, overcome adversity, build resilience and increase joy by intensifying your desire, and increasing your ability to cope with stress, setbacks and disappointment.

You've discovered ways to feeding your soul and achieve your highest potential—following your passion, jumping with joy and bouncing high...and more.

Positive health behaviours including journaling, meditation, regular exercise, good diet, relaxation exercises, and rest are a few of the many techniques we've covered.

Listed below are some helpful reminders of some of the many holistic coping strategies you can call upon during times of current or anticipated need.

Physical

- Learn to listen to your body
- Adequate exercise

- Physical touch/massage
- Muscle relaxation
- Sleep
- Warmth
- Relaxation breathing
- Healthy diet, i.e. reducing stimulants (coffee, nicotine etc.), increasing water, and eating organic non-processed foods
- Yoga

BEHAVIOURAL

- Balanced lifestyle
- Support groups / Counseling
- Sharing with friends and family
- Humor
- New interests / activities
- Hobbies
- Socializing
- Entertaining
- Taking time out
- Music / dancing / singing/creative expression
- Meditating
- Yoga
- Being proactive and taking control of the situation
- Change careers
- Reducing or eliminating alcohol consumption
- Making time to do nothing at all

COGNITIVE / Perceptual (thinking)

- Rational thinking techniques to help change the way you interpret the stressful situation
- Positive thinking/cultivating optimism
- Self-assertion training
- Personal development
- Building self-esteem
- Realistic goal planning
- Time management
- Learning to say "No"
- Priority clarification
- Reflection
- Mindfulness
- Acceptance
- Hypnosis

Emotional

- Releasing emotions and expressing feelings (laugh, talk, cry, write in a journal, paint etc.)
- Learning how to "switch off"
- Taking time out
- Solitude and space
- Intimacy
- Counseling and support
- Challenging your emotional reactions to situations
- Passion/Joy

Social

- Scheduling time to spend with important people in your life
- Making plans with friends, family and loved ones in advance
- Sharing your experiences of stress with certain people in your life, especially letting them know the ways that stress has been affecting you, so they understand
- Practicing assertive communication within your significant relationships to decrease conflicts, while also continuing to find ways to show people around you that they are important

Spiritual

- Prayer and mediation—scheduling regular time
- Helping others (talking, writing, supporting)
- Reiki and other energy healing techniques
- Talking with a spiritual confidant or leader to explain any spiritual issues or doubts that you may have encountered
- Forgiveness (of self or others)
- Compassion / loving kindness
- Continuing to read and learn about your faith, belief or value system
- Connecting with others who share your beliefs

A FEW LAST WORDS

I hope this book has provided encouragement and empowered your tenacity to succeed. The world news more love, more creative people, more beauty in this world—in short, the world needs you.

Adopt a millionaire mindset—don't settle. Dream big, be audacious, take inspired action, and fear less. The power to live a significant life lies within you.

Counting your blessings and remember to be happy and thankful for even the simplest, and often the most valuable, things. These may include:

- Enjoying good health and mobility
- Being loved and loving in return
- Tapping into your infinite potential
- The ability to say, think, do, and create what you truly feel
- The ability to enchant and inspire others with your words
- Healing the world—one creative step at a time
- Inspiring others with your courage
- Feeling happy with yourself
- Fulfilment
- Living authentically

- Being audacious

... Or something else.

What matters most is not how you overcome obstacles to success. What matters is how meaningful the end result is for you.

Take care of yourself and your heart, and nourish your mind, body and soul.

If you continue to exercise self-care and bounce with joy and child-like curiosity through life, and adapt a spirit of playfulness through challenging times, then this unknown and unpredictable creative life will manifest in favorable outcomes—for you, for those you love, and those drawn to you because of the beauty, power, and magic of what you create.

You may think the outcome has to happen in a certain way, on a certain day, but you can't always predict how life will bounce. Human willpower cannot make everything happen. Spirit has its own idea, of how the arrow flies, and upon which wind it travels.

It may not happen overnight, but if you follow your heart, maintain your focus, and take inspired action, your time will come.

I promise!

If by some strange twist of fate, it doesn't, at least you'll know you tried. A life of no regrets—now that's worth striving for.

Let the beauty you love be the life that you live.

Now go forth and create!

TO YOUR HAPPINESS AND JOY, and with love,

P.S. I truly hoped your enjoyed *The Happy, Healthy Artist*. I'm excited about the possibilities to take this simple but profound message of resilience and joy out into the world. Everyone needs encouragement and help to keep bouncing through life—especially we sensitive souls.

SIGN up for my newsletter to be the first to know when new books are released, and receive practical tips to live your best life here >>

Be the first to know when my guided meditations and self-hypnosis audios are released, and stay tuned for news of my online courses, webinars and international retreats in exotic, empowering locations.

Sign up here http://eepurl.com/bEArfT

ALSO BY CASSANDRA GAISFORD

Transformational Super Kids:

The Little Princess
The Little Princess Can Fly
I Have to Grow
The Boy Who Cried

Mid-Life Career Rescue:

The Call for Change
What Makes You Happy
Employ Yourself
Job Search Strategies That Work
3 Book Box Set: The Call for Change, What Makes You Happy, Employ Yourself
4 Book Box Set: The Call for Change, What Makes You Happy, Employ Yourself, Job Search Strategies That Work

Career Change:

ALSO BY CASSANDRA GAISFORD

Career Change 2020 5 Book-Bundle Box Set

Master Life Coach:

Leonardo da Vinci: Life Coach
Coco Chanel: Life Coach

The Art of Living:

How to Find Your Passion and Purpose
How to Find Your Passion and Purpose Companion Workbook
Career Rescue: The Art and Science of Reinventing Your Career and Life
Boost Your Self-Esteem and Confidence
Anxiety Rescue
No! Why 'No' is the New 'Yes'
How to Find Your Joy and Purpose
How to Find Your Joy and Purpose Companion Workbook

The Art of Success:

Leonardo da Vinci
Coco Chanel

Journaling Prompts Series:

The Passion Journal
The Passion-Driven Business Planning Journal
How to Find Your Passion and Purpose 2 Book-Bundle Box Set

Health & Happiness:

The Happy, Healthy Artist
Stress Less. Love Life More
Bounce: Overcoming Adversity, Building Resilience and Finding Joy
Bounce Companion Workbook

ALSO BY CASSANDRA GAISFORD

Mindful Sobriety:

Mind Your Drink: The Surprising Joy of Sobriety
Mind Over Mojitos: How Moderating Your Drinking Can Change Your Life: Easy Recipes for Happier Hours & a Joy-Filled Life
Your Beautiful Brain: Control Alcohol and Love Life More

Happy Sobriety:

Happy Sobriety: Non-Alcoholic Guilt-Free Drinks You'll Love
The Sobriety Journal
Happy Sobriety Two Book Bundle-Box Set: Alcohol and Guilt-Free Drinks You'll Love & The Sobriety Journal

Money Manifestation:

Financial Rescue: The Total Money Makeover: Create Wealth, Reduce Debt & Gain Freedom

The Prosperous Author:

Developing a Millionaire Mindset
Productivity Hacks: Do Less & Make More
Two Book Bundle-Box Set (Books 1-2)

Miracle Mindset:

Change Your Mindset: Millionaire Mindset Makeover: The Power of Purpose, Passion, & Perseverance

Non-Fiction:

Where is Salvator Mundi?

More of Cassandra's practical and inspiring workbooks on a range of

ALSO BY CASSANDRA GAISFORD

career and life-enhancing topics are on her website (www.cassandragaisford.com) and her author page at all good online bookstores.

COACHING AND WELLNESS THERAPIES

If you could free yourself from everything holding you back from living an incredible life —all of your fears, stinkin' thinking, limiting beliefs, negative emotions —you know you'd instantly feel happier, healthier and freer, right? But how? How can you liberate yourself from all that obstacles and blocks preventing you from living your best life?

The solution is so simple. Whether you have lost your job or hate the one you have, your relationship has hit a rough patch, or you're struggling with anxiety, depression, addiction or any other issues are impacting your life, talking to an impartial professional, qualified holistic therapist, counselor, and life coach can help.

I offer a range of transformational life and career rescue remedies, including:

• **Quantum Transformational Coaching** (*QTC*) to rapidly breakthrough limiting beliefs, sabotaging thoughts, subconscious blocks, and outdated scripts that are holding you back.

• **Akashic Records Soul Reading**—Unlock your destiny, heal the past, manifest a wonderful future. Achieve truly transformational and life-changing results fast.

• **Career Counselling** to help resolve career-related issues such as stress, role-conflict, job loss, workplace bullying, dissatisfaction, and assistance with career reinvention planning and self-employment coaching,

• **Personal therapy** provides early, solutions-focused intervention before problems escalate. A holistic approach to resolving many non-work issues including relationships, finances, physical and emotional well-being stress, grief, conflict, depression, lack of self-esteem, substance abuse…and more.

• Life coaching to help you when you don't need in-depth counseling. You may just be feeling stuck, lost, or demotivated, and need someone objective and supportive (and sometimes bossy!) to spur you on. Life coaching is solutions-focused, and rather than dwell on the past, focuses on where you are now, where you want to be and the steps and changes necessary to get you there

Live and work with purpose, passion, and prosperity no matter where you are in New Zealand or the world. I can help you reach your potential by phone, Skype or by e-mail. Schedule an appointment here—I'd love to provide guidance and support to help you live your best life.

Or, navigate to the following page to learn more about my wellness therapies and coaching services and how they can help you:

http://www.cassandragaisford.com/wellness-therapies/

"Thank YOU! Our coaching was immensely helpful, and I have renewed hope for finding my way. You are simply lovely, and brilliant, and wise. So glad our energies aligned, and I found you! I am also so enjoying your books and will give more feedback as I go as well as post reviews online. And they will be GLOWING, I can assure you!"

~ Lisa Webb, artist

"A coaching session with Cassandra is like a light switch to a light bulb. My ideas were there but without that light switch I wasn't able to see them and manifest my dream of running a holistic business from home. Straight away, Cassandra was able to get to the heart of my core values and how to put them into a dream business. I now have the sense of purpose and drive to achieve my business goals. Cassandra's warm personality and positive approach make her a joy to work with. I recommend her to anyone who wants to unlock their personal and professional potential."

~ Shelley Sweeney, writer & Reiki practitioner

(Did you know that coaching fees are often tax deductible for people who use coaching to improve their professional skills? Check with your accountant for details.)

FOLLOW YOUR PASSION TO PROSPERITY ONLINE COURSE

If you need more help to find and live your life purpose you may prefer to take my online course, and watch inspirational and practical videos and other strategies to help you to fulfill your potential.

Follow your passion and purpose to prosperity—online coaching program

Easily discover your passion and purpose, overcoming barriers to success, and create a job or business you love with my self-paced online course.

Gain unlimited lifetime access to this course, for as long as you like—across any and all devices you own. Be supported with practical, inspirational, easy-to-access strategies to achieve your dreams.

To start achieving outstanding personal and professional results with absolute certainty and excitement. **Click here to enrol or find out more—the-coaching-lab.teachable.com/p/follow-your-passion-and-purpose-to-prosperity**

FURTHER RESOURCES

SURF THE NET

Mathew Johnstone has a wide range of books and resources on mental wellness and mindfulness: www.matthewjohnstone.com.au

www.whatthebleep.com—a powerful and inspiring site emphasizing quantum physics and the transformational power of thought.

www.heartmath.org—comprehensive information and tools help you access your intuitive insight and heart-based knowledge. Validated and supported by science-based research. Check out the additional information about your heart-brain.

Join polymath Tim Ferris and learn from his interesting and informative guests on The Tim Ferris Show http://fourhourworkweek.com/podcast/.

Listen to podcasts which inspire you to become the best version of your writing self—*Joanna Penn's podcast* is very helpful for "authorpreneurs" http://www.thecreativepenn.com/podcasts. I also love Neil

FURTHER RESOURCES

Patel's podcast for savvy marketing strategies http://neilpatel.com/podcast.

Experience the transformative power of hypnosis. One of my favorite hypnosis sites is the UK-based Uncommon Knowledge. On their website http://www.hypnosisdownloads.com you'll find a range of self-hypnosis mp3 audios, including The Millionaire Mindset program.

Celebrity hypnotherapist and author Marissa Peer is another favorite source of subconscious reprogramming and liberation —www.marisapeer.com.

What beliefs are holding you back? Check out Peer's Youtube clip "How To Teach Your Mind That Everything Is Available To You" here —https://www.youtube.com/watch?v=IKeaAbM2kJg

Enjoy James Clear's fabulous blog content and receive further self-improvement tips based on proven scientific research: http://jamesclear.com/articles

Tim Ferriss recommends a couple of apps for those wanting some help getting started with meditation—Headspace (www.headspace.com) or Calm (www.calm.com).

National Geographic: The Science of Stress: Portrait of a killer
https://www.youtube.com/watch?v=ZyBsy5SQxqU

Effects of Stress on Your Body
https://www.youtube.com/watch?v=1p6EeYwp1O4

Mindfulness training
Wellington-based Peter Fernando offers an introductory guided meditation which you can take further. He also meets with individuals and groups in Wellington for philosophical talks on mindfulness and Buddhism. Very enjoyable and great for the soul.

http://www.monthofmindfulness.info

Guided meditations
www.calm.com

Free app with guided meditations
http://eocinstitute.org/meditation/emotional-benefits-of-meditation/
Includes a comprehensive list of the benefits of meditation.

Career Guidance Sites:
www.aarp.org/work - information and tools to help you stay current and connected with what's hot and what's not in today's workplace.

www.lifereimagined.org - loads of inspiration and practical tips to help you maximize your interests and expertise, personalized and interactive.

www.whatthebleep.com – a powerful and inspiring site emphasizing quantum physics and the transformational power of thought.

www.personalitytype.com—created by the authors of *Do What You Are: Discover the Perfect Career for You through the Secrets of Personality Type*. This site focuses on expanding your awareness of your own type and that of others—including children and partners. This site also contains many useful links.

BOOKS

Master your millionaire mindset with T. Harv Eker's book, *Secrets of the Millionaire Mind: Mastering the Inner Game of Wealth*.

Find your ONE thing with Gary Keller in *The One Thing: The Surprisingly Simple Truth Behind Extraordinary Results*.

Learn from masters in a diverse cross-section of fields—pick up a copy of Tim Ferriss' *Tool of Titans*.

Celebrate being an outlier and learn why clocking up 10,000 hours

FURTHER RESOURCES

will help you succeed in Malcolm Gladwell's *Outliers: The Story of Success.*

Struggling in an extroverted world? Introverts are enjoying a renaissance, fueled in part by Susan Cain's terrific bestseller, *Quiet: The Power of Introverts in a World That Can't Stop Talking.*

Copy-cat your way to success with Austin Kleon's great book, *Steal Like An Artist.*

Roll up your sleeves and bring out the big guns to win your creative battle with *The War of Art* by Steven Pressfield.

Power up with a new personality—read Breaking the Habit of Being Yourself: How to Lose Your Mind and Create a New One by Dr. Joe Dispenza.

Unleash the power of your mind by reading *You Are the Placebo: Making Your Mind Matter,* by Dr. Joe Dispenza.

Manifest your prosperity with Rhonda Byrne in her popular book, *The Secret.*

Ensure you don't starve by reading Jeff Goins collated wisdom in *Real Artists Don't Starve: Timeless Strategies for Thriving in the New Creative Age.*

Fortify your faith with Julia Cameron's book, *Faith and Will.*

How to Survive and Thrive in Any Life Crisis, Dr. Al Siebert

Thrive: The Third Metric to Redefining Success and Creating a Happier Life, Arianna Huffington

(This book has great content throughout and some excellent resources listed in the back.)

The Power of Now: A Guide to Spiritual Enlightenment, Eckhart Tolle

The Book of Joy, The Dalai Lama and Archbishop Desmond Tutu

The Sleep Revolution: Transforming Your Life One Night at a Time, Arianna Huffington

Quiet the Mind: An Illustrated Guide on How to Meditate, Mathew Johnstone

Comfortable with Uncertainty: 108 Teachings on Cultivating Fearlessness and Compassion, Pema Chodron

Power vs. Force: The Hidden Determinants of Human Behavior, David R. Hawkins

FURTHER RESOURCES

Learn how to live an inspired life with Tarot cards and other oracles. Read Jessa Crispin's book, *The Creative Tarot: A Modern Guide to an Inspired Life.*

Check out all of Collette-Baron-Reid's books, including: *Uncharted: The Journey Through Uncertainty to Infinite Possibility* and *Messages from Spirit: The Extraordinary Power of Oracles, Omens, and Signs.*

PLEASE LEAVE A REVIEW

Word of mouth is the most powerful marketing force in the universe. If you found this book useful, I'd appreciate you rating this book and leaving a review. You don't have to say much—just a few words about how the book helped you learn something new or made you feel.

"Your books are a fantastic resource and until now I never even thought to write a review. Going forward I will be reviewing more books. So many great ones out there and I want to support the amazing people that write them."
Great reviews help people find good books.

Thank you so much! I appreciate you!

PS: If you enjoyed this book, do me a small favour to help spread the word about it and share on Facebook, Twitter and other social networks.

ABOUT THE AUTHOR

Cassandra Gaisford, is a holistic therapist, award-winning artist, and #1 bestselling author. A corporate escapee, she now lives and works from her idyllic lifestyle property overlooking the Bay of Islands in New Zealand.

Cassandra is best known for the passionate call to redefine what it means to be successful in today's world.

She is a well-known expert in the area of success, passion, purpose and transformational business, career and life change, and is regularly sought after as a keynote speaker, and by media seeking an expert opinion on career and personal development issues.

Cassandra has also contributed to international publications and been interviewed on national radio and television in New Zealand and America.

She has a proven-track record of success helping people find savvy ways to boost their finances, change careers, build a business or become a solopreneur—on a shoestring.

Cassandra's unique blend of business experience and qualifications (BCA, Dip Psych.), creative skills, and well-ness and holistic training (Dip Counselling, Reiki Master Teacher) blends pragmatism and commercial savvy with rare and unique insight and out-of-the-box-thinking for anyone wanting to achieve an extraordinary life.

Learn more about her on her website, her blog, or connect with her on Facebook and Twitter.

ACKNOWLEDGMENTS

This book (and my new life) was made possible by the amazing generosity, open heartedness, and wonderful friendship of so many people. Thank you!

Sir Edmund Hillary often said that even Mount Everest wasn't climbed alone. A great achievement, or in my case a good book, is a product of collaboration. This project has, at times, loomed larger than the highest mountain in the world. I could not have persevered without the tremendous encouragement from a wealth of supportive and talented people.

To all the amazingly interesting clients who have allowed me to help them over the years, and to the wonderful people who read my newspaper columns and wrote to me with their stories of reinvention—thank you. Your feedback, deep sharing, requests for help, and inspired, courageous action continues to inspire me.

I'd also like to say a special thanks to the staff at *The Dominion Post* newspaper who gave me my first break into published writing. This book would never have existed had they not acted on my suggestion that a careers column would be a great idea. For over four years they gave me the encouragement and artistic freedom to write freely on a range of topics—all with the goal of helping to encourage and inspire others.

I'm also grateful to the Health Editor of *Marie Claire* magazine whom, after she had accepted a short article, said I had the bones of a good book and should write it.

A huge thank you also to my amazing authorpreneurs including Melinda Hammond, Barry Watson, Courtney Kenney, Paul Brodie, Dustin Heiner, Joanna Just, Mimi Emmanuel, Kylie Ansett, Scott Allan, Heidi Farrelly, Marjory Harris, Nick Daniel, Davina Chessid, and so many others. I am so grateful for your support and the generous sharing of talent within the Authorpreneur Mastermind Group.

Cate Walker, once again, for your beautiful and thorough editing.

Thank you also to the advance readers who provided additional feedback and suggested improvements—I am truly blessed to have received your input and cheerleading.

But importantly, thank YOU for purchasing this book. I look forward to your feedback and hearing news of your success.

xxx

STAY IN TOUCH

Become a fan and Continue To Be Supported, Encouraged, and Inspired

Subscribe to my newsletter and follow me on BookBub (https://www.bookbub.com/profile/cassandra-gaisford) and be the first to know about my new releases and giveaways

www.cassandragaisford.com
www.facebook.com/powerfulcreativity
www.instagram.com/cassandragaisford
www.youtube.com/cassandragaisfordnz
www.pinterest.com/cassandraNZ
www.linkedin.com/in/cassandragaisford
www.twitter.com/cassandraNZ

And please, do check out some of my videos where I share strategies and tips to stress less and love life more—http://www.youtube.com/cassandragaisfordnz

STAY IN TOUCH

BLOG

Subscribe and be inspired by regular posts to help you increase your wellness, follow your bliss, slay self-doubt, and sustain healthy habits.

Learn more about how to achieve happiness and success at work and life by visiting my blog:

www.cassandragaisford.com/archives

SPEAKING EVENTS

Cassandra is available internationally for speaking events aimed at wellness strategies, motivation, inspiration and as a keynote speaker.

She has an enthusiastic, humorous and passionate style of delivery and is celebrated for her ability to motivate, inspire and enlighten.

For information navigate to www.cassandragaisford.com/contact/speaking

To ask Cassandra to come and speak at your workplace or conference, contact: cassandra@cassandragaisford.com

NEWSLETTERS

For inspiring tools and helpful tips subscribe to Cassandra's free newsletters here:
http://www.cassandragaisford.com

Sign up now and receive a free eBook to help you find your passion and purpose!

STAY IN TOUCH

http://eepurl.com/bEArfT

EXCERPT: THE PROSPEROUS AUTHOR

THE PROSPEROUS AUTHOR:

How to Make a Living with Your Writing

Book One: Developing A Millionaire Mindset

Cassandra Gaisford, BCA, Dip Psych

Available now in paperback and eBook

PRAISE FOR THE PROSPEROUS AUTHOR

"What I really like about *The Prosperous Author* is that it is a great book to read before you even put pen to paper. There are a zillion books on the market which tell us how to market and publish our books. This book stands apart from the rest in that it gets your head in the right mindset to create the best possible book.

The Prosperous Author is overflowing with wonderful, motivating and thought-provoking quotes from bestselling and award-winning authors as samples and inspiration. This may be Cassandra's finest book yet."

~ Mimi Emmanuel, author of *The Holy Grail of Book Publishing*

"Cassandra Gaisford has molded a helpful resource in her latest publication *The Prosperous Author.* Together with helpful ideas encouraging readers to believe in their writing, or in my case in my project, she also presents challenges to motivate the reader, well-chosen examples of successful writers, and honest offerings of her own journey.

This book provides well-researched ideas to support anyone who has a dream to believe in themselves and go for gold and develop that dream into reality. It is not just for writers, it is for all of us who have a golden nugget of a dream and want to bring it to full creation."

~ Catherine Sloan, counselor

"A lot of great insights on how to become a more positive, passionate and prosperous writer. I loved the second part of the book, 'Cultivate a Burning Desire.' It really motivates me and inspires me to see how successful writers think and act. I like the resources and ideas Cassandra Gaisford gave throughout. There were also some great quotes that I liked a lot. I'll definitely refer back to this book in the future to assist me on my personal journey to become a prosperous writer!"

~ Thibaut Meurisse, blogger

"Author Cassandra Gaisford has brought a much needed book to the self-publishing market. The author of the popular *Mid-Life Career Rescue* series has published multiple books on Amazon and is now sharing her secrets as a successful author in this latest book, *The Prosperous Author: How to Make a Living With Your Writing*.

The Prosperous Author is a great read that really dives into the mindset of what it means to not just prosper financially but to live a successful and well-balanced life based on health, happiness and close relationships. This book is definitely for the reader who lacks self-esteem and wants more of it, wants to overcome perfectionism, or has doubt and uncertainty and needs to break beyond these barriers. *The Prosperous Author* can show you how to do all of that.

This book really has a positive impact on one's mindset. As the author points out in her key message throughout the book, mindset is at the core of all our success. It creates emotion and motivation. It brings us up or keeps us down.

The book wastes no time and jumps right into 'the millionaire mindset.' We can learn how to think like a millionaire and how to develop the strategies and apply them to our life for attracting more influence and money. By programming your subconscious beliefs, you are rewiring your own brain for success. The author teaches us to nurture our thoughts and cast out the negative seeds that are growing there. We can see that attitude is everything.

Energy is another great topic discussed. We can boost our energy by cutting away the relationships and negative influences holding us back. This is one of my favorite chapters in the book. We can 'relive our life story' too, by imagining the life that we could have instead of the life that we wished we had had. Then, in the chapter 'Blossom,' we learn to pay attention to divine creativity, intuition, and signs of manifestation.

Cassandra gets into the topic of passion and we can see how cultivating a passionate lifestyle frees us up to pursue life's gifts; and to craft our writing into a solid piece of reading material. Write with your purpose and the words will flow much easier.

This book really hits home for me as an author *and* someone who is dedicated to carving out purpose, passion and a life of more wealth and health. Every chapter ends with a positive wrap-up ['Mining for Gold'] of the important lessons learned.

The other great chapters will teach you how to:

Dream big, create a new destiny and turn a profit as a successful author. My favorite chapters here are:

Keeping deadlines. Without deadlines, how can we get our work finished? There are solid strategies here for doing just that. As Cassandra points out as well, we can become prosperous authors by journaling our way to success, staying focused on the task, keeping doubt out, sticking with perseverance, and believing in yourself to get the job done.

This book is well-written, structured and serves as an excellent resource for authors and people looking to fill up their lives with positivity for achieving their goals and objectives.

A definite 'Good Read' recommendation."

~ Scott Allan, author of *Do It Scared*

For Lorenzo
whose mantra
"Show me the money!"
inspires me to succeed.

EPILOGUE

There Will Come a Moment...

When your life begins to unfold with new and wonderful events, there will come a moment that you will be in awe, wonder, and utter wakefulness when you realize it was your mind that created them. In your rapture, you will look back from this vantage point at your entire life, and you will not want to change anything. You will not regret any action or feel bad about whatever has happened to you, because in that moment of your manifestation, it will all make sense to you. You will see how your past got you to this great state.

~ Dr. Joe Dispenza, author

AUTHOR'S NOTE

I've been a published non-fiction writer for over ten years, penning articles for newspapers and magazines. Most of the time I wrote for free. My motivation? I wanted to provide helpful tips and strategies for people who couldn't afford my coaching and psychology fees.

I also started writing inspirational workbooks for career and life coaching clients who were sent to me for help by their workplaces—but only given two or three paid hours of support. Early on, before Kindle became the phenomenon that it is now, I began thinking of ways I could help more people with my words of self-help and empowerment.

The editor of *Marie Claire* Magazine suggested I write a book. The first book I wrote, *Happy at Work for Mid-Lifers,* was turned down by so many publishing houses that I began to get discouraged. They told me, "New Zealander's aren't ready for passion. It won't sell." I knew they were wrong. So, I decided to back myself and start my own self-publishing company and self-publish. I've since written and released numerous non-fiction books and branched into fiction too—writing romance novels under my pen name Mollie Mathews.

I have self-published over 20 titles in the last two years alone—all

AUTHOR'S NOTE

them have been #1 bestsellers on Amazon. I have created multiple streams of income—many of them from my writing. Others from my work as a holistic psychologist and coach and also from certifying people to become Worklife Solutions life and career coaches.

People write to me and tell me that are awed by my prosperous productivity and success. But I feel it's so important to let you know that I wasn't always the confident, prosperous author I am today.

For many years I struggled to complete the books I wanted to write. I wrestled unsuccessfully with doubt and fear and other blocks to living a prosperous writing life.

Because of my own limiting beliefs about my writing and my ability to make money as a writer, it took me until my sixteenth book to call myself an author. Even then I struggled. I hadn't gone to University and received an English degree, I didn't train as a journalist. Everything I learned was self-taught.

Happily, I'm a compulsive note-taker and researcher—my partner once said that I'm an obsessive collector of positivity. My goal has always been to overcome obstacles and live my best life—and to help other people achieve the same.

Whenever I'm in a slump or needing an inspirational boost, I turn to people who are smarter or more skilled than me for good advice. Very often, I write a book to self-help my way to prosperity.

If you've been procrastinating, experiencing self-doubt, feeling fearful, or just getting in your own way, you're in good company. I've been there, too—as have many successful people. Guess what, getting in your own way is normal!

I promise there are solutions to the problems you're currently facing—and you'll find them in the pages that follow.

Much of the wisdom contained in this book, the first in The Prosperity for Authors series, derives from the success strategies I've distilled and applied in the last few years—having finally "knocked the buggers off" (to paraphrase one of the first people to climb the summit of Mount Everest, and fellow New Zealander, Sir Edmund Hillary).

AUTHOR'S NOTE

As I've already said, after years of starting books and never finishing them, in the past two years I've written, finished, and published twenty bestselling books.

What changed?

My mindset—amongst other things.

In The Prosperity for Authors series, I'll share with you the things I've learned figuring out how to make a living from my writing.

You'll benefit from dozens of insights based on survey research and my professional achievements as a holistic psychologist, bestselling author, and creativity expert.

You'll gain insight into the success secrets of extraordinary authors and creative entrepreneurs from a variety of fiction and non-fiction genres. Tim Ferriss, James Patterson, Paulo Coelho, Nora Roberts, Arianna Huffington, Oprah, and Isabel Allende are just a few of the many creative mentors you'll learn from.

As you'll discover, being prosperous is not just about money; it's also about health, happiness, close relationships, living a meaningful life, and enjoying life's journey.

- If you'd love to find a way to create a living from your writing
- If you suffer from self-doubt or fear of failure
- If you need approval from others
- If you lack confidence or self-esteem
- If you're a perfectionist or find the challenges of a creative life overwhelming
- Or, if you've already embarked on the writer's journey and want to elevate your success

. . . then *The Prosperous Author: Developing A Millionaire Mindset* is exactly the right book for you. It will show you that these challenges, obstacles, and desires are a critical part of your success.

If you'd like to make a living from your writing, developing a prosperous mindset is the foundation skill from which all else follows.

AUTHOR'S NOTE

The ideas described in this book apply to anyone who's trying to inject some prosperous creativity into their life and work.

In short, this book is for you—whoever you are, whatever you ache to create, and however you define prosperity.

INTRODUCTION

...Mindset. There's no getting away from it: that's a crucial part of the puzzle.

~ Mark Dawson, author

"Real artists don't starve," writes Jeff Goins in his latest book titled by the same name.

It's a confronting statement—in part because it's true. Some of the most successful authors today are making serious coin from their writing.

Former welfare beneficiary J.K. Rowling is a millionaire many times over. James Patterson, the son of an insurance salesman, earns so much he was able to donate over $26 million US dollars to institutions supporting higher learning.

But Goins' assertion is confronting because it's also untrue.

Historical archives are littered with the failure stories of talented, prolific, memorable writers and artists who never experienced financial success in their lifetimes.

Vincent Van Gogh never earned a sustainable living and was often destitute.

INTRODUCTION

F. Scott Fitzgerald, once one of the highest paid authors of his generation, died an impoverished, discouraged alcoholic.

As Goins notes in *Real Artists Don't Starve*, "At the time of Fitzgerald's death, *The Great Gatsby* was practically out of print and nowhere to be found in bookstores. His last royalty check was for thirteen dollars, most of which was from copies the author had purchased himself. A once-promising novelist ended his career doing what he considered hack work and went to the grave thinking himself a failure."

Poet and novelist Edgar Allan Poe, credited by many as being the inventor of the detective fiction genre, died penniless.

Oscar Wilde, the flamboyant writer, poet and playwright, was forced into bankruptcy.

And then there are the vast numbers of aspiring authors you'll never hear of who have suffered financially pursuing their dream of making a living from their writing.

Nearly everyone wants to be rich. So, why do only a few reach those heights? How do millions of writers work their fingers to the bone yet end up broke?

...and others don't?

It's not about luck.

Many millionaire authors will tell you that luck played a large part in their success. They hit the right idea at the right time in the right place—and you could stop there, assuming that unless you get lucky, you won't get rich.

But then if you look a little deeper, you'll uncover something else, something all prosperous people have in common—the millionaire mindset.

And even more interestingly, millionaires don't have much else in common—there's no standard for academic achievement; there's no commonality of family background; there's no "special knowledge" that these people possess.

It's about your mindset.

INTRODUCTION

When it comes down to it, success flows from the habits, attitudes and behaviors you use *every day* that move you, step-by-step, towards millionaire status.

And yes, sometimes even the rich go belly up, but something they never lose is their millionaire mindset.

What is a millionaire mindset?

- Millionaires think big; they may start off with small goals, but they always have a big goal in mind
- Millionaires aren't afraid to fail. They play to win, not to avoid defeat
- Millionaires focus on what they want—and go for it
- Millionaires are goal-orientated
- Millionaires focus on growth; they know comfort stunts progress
- Millionaires look to monetize everything
- Millionaires accumulate money; sometimes they appear stingy, but they know being frugal is the way to grow their bank balance
- Millionaires never stop learning; they pursue greatness and they invest in continual improvement
- Millionaires learn from their mistakes
- Millionaires maintain a positive mindset
- Millionaires know that success attracts success; they learn from and surround themselves with only the best
- Millionaires enjoy attention—if not on themselves personally, then on their brand. They're tireless self-promoters and know that attention attracts money

By thinking like a millionaire and applying the success secrets of highly successful authors, you'll maximize your likelihood of success.

Your goal may not be to make millions—your goal may be to enjoy following your passion for telling stories and to have fun doing it.

You may wish to earn a small living from your writing—or a grand

INTRODUCTION

one. You may wish to prepare your mindset for the day you decide to tackle your writing project.

Whatever your intention, in this book you'll learn how to develop a winning mindset so that you thrive, not just survive, as an author.

Although this book was written for writers, the principles and strategies can be embraced by business entrepreneurs, actors, dancers, painters, photographers, filmmakers, and thousands of others around the world who want to enhance their mindsets.

YOUR 5-STEP BLUEPRINT TO TRUE SUCCESS

It takes a certain amount of discipline. I guarantee you that it is the discipline that will pay off.

~ James Patterson, author

Developing a prosperous mindset is the foundation skill from which all else follows.

The first book in The Prosperity for Authors series, *How to Make a Living from your Writing: Developing a Millionaire Mindset*, takes a holistic look at what it means, and what it takes to develop, a prosperous mindset.

Through inspiring anecdotes of successful creatives both past and present, and by following the 5-Step Blueprint to True Success, you'll discover that making a living from your writing is not only doable, it's also a fulfilling way to live an extraordinary life.

The Five Principles of Prosperity

I've sectioned *Developing a Millionaire Mindset* into clusters of principles. Principles aren't constricting rules incapable of being shaped, but rather general and fundamental truths which may be used to help guide your choices.

Let's look briefly at the five principles of prosperity and what each will cover:

INTRODUCTION

The only way to change your 'outer' world is to first change your 'inner' world. The first step in developing a prosperous mindset is learning how to master the inner game of wealth.

Principle One will teach you how to train your brain to think like a millionaire and program your mind for success.

You'll also discover why a holistic approach to creating a successful writing career is an important part of achieving prosperity.

Principle Two will show you how to intensify your desire, harness the power of passion and purpose, and dream big to elevate your success.

Principle Three will help you shift gears by thinking and acting like a pro. Professionals love numbers, plan for success, finish what they start, and work smart.

Your health is the cornerstone of your wealth, yet it's an area many creatives devalue—until they get a wake-up call. Start smart and invest in healthy routines—you'll learn how in **Principle Four**.

Principle Five will begin the process of slaying any obstacles to success, including unhelpful beliefs, doubt, and sabotaging subconscious scripts that keep you stuck.

In this book you'll learn:

- The secrets to developing a prosperous mindset
- How to define prosperity on your own terms
- How to master the psychology of creation
- How to unlock your potential
- How to overcome the fears that stop you from reaching your fullest potential
- How to fight through your blocks and win your inner creative battles
- How to set and achieve audacious goals
- How to steal from your heroes (rather than waiting for inspiration)
- How to take strategic risks (rather than reckless ones)
- How to overcome your fear of failure, criticism, and change

INTRODUCTION

- How to whip anxiety, despondency and depression into shape
- How to overcome inertia, writer's block, and the resistance of a blank page
- How to identify real priorities that are central to your life and to define work's true meaning
- How to turn pro, tap your inner power, and create your life's work

But mostly what I hope you will gain from this book is encouragement, inspiration, and stimulation if you are, or ever hope to be, a writer.

HOW TO USE THIS BOOK

Think of *The Prosperous Author* like a shot of espresso. Sometimes one quick hit is all it takes to get started. But sometimes you need a few shots to sustain your energy. Or maybe you need a bigger motivational hit and then you're on your way.

You're in control of what works best for you. Go at your own pace, but resist over-caffeinating. A little bit of guidance here and there can do as much to fast-track your success as consuming all the principles in one hit.

Skim to sections that are most relevant to you, and return to familiar ground to reinforce home-truths. But most of all, enjoy your experience.

Mining for Gold

Apply the principles which follow by journaling your responses to the questions and challenges presented at the end of each chapter.

"I love your works to date—provocative and supportive at the same time," a gentleman who'd read my *Mid-Life Career Rescue* books wrote to me.

To provoke is to incite or stimulate. It's the reason I've included open-ended questions and calls to action in each guide. The best questions are open, generative ones that don't allow for "yes/no" answers; rather, they encourage you to tap into your higher wisdom and intuition, or to go in search of answers—as successful people do.

"I really like the questions at the end of each chapter—'Mining for Gold.' They challenge my thinking; they provide me with opportunities to move forward with my own project; and overall they bring a well-rounded focus to what has been written in the preceding section/chapter," a reader of this book wrote to me.

Dive Deeper with *The Prosperous Author Workbook*

The Prosperous Author will also be available as a printed workbook, with space to write your responses to the challenges and calls to action within the book.

Expand Your Learning—Follow My Blog

Dive deeper into some of the insights I've shared and sign up for my newsletter at http://eepurl.com/cQXY4f and follow my blog—navigate to www.cassandragaisford.com.

Re-read My Other Books

"Re-reading books has been one of my secrets to success, because more often than not, I miss some (or most) of the good stuff the first time around," says Bryan Cohen, author and co-creator of the "Sell More Books Show" (sellmorebooksshow.com).

Cohen continues, "Even if I caught the goodies on read number one, it's very possible I didn't *apply* the information to my career or actually *complete* the exercises within."

Have you ever been guilty of skipping over the exercises in a book or failing to experiment and try some of its tips and strategy methods? I know I have.

That's why I think you should re-read not just my books, but any others you found inspiring.

Visit the link below to go to my Amazon author's page and remind yourself of the books you've already read—or would love to read —Author.to/CassandraGaisford.

INTRODUCTION

Inspirational Quotes to Support and Empower

Sometimes all it takes is one encouraging word, one timely bit of advice to awaken your power within. Throughout *The Prosperous Author* I've added a variety of short sound-bites of wisdom—choosing from a wide range of super-capable men and women, historical and current, young and old.

They are men and women who share your dreams and had to overcome significant obstacles on the way to prosperity and success.

Be Empowered

Empowerment is defined as giving power or authority to someone or something—who better to decide who assumes this power and sovereign authority than you.

Empowered people do what they need to do to assume mastery over their thoughts, feelings, emotions, and things that affect their lives.

Empowered people are successful people because they live life on their own terms; they do the things that really matter to them and those they love.

Empowered people are resilient in the face of setbacks, disappointments, or attacks, and they're flexible enough to tackle obstacles in their paths.

They recognize that they are the experts and sovereign authority in their lives. They learn from, and surround themselves with, other empowered, successful people. They back themselves even when they don't succeed.

Are you ready to heed the call for prosperity?

Let's get going...

YOUR MILLIONAIRE MIND

1

WHAT IS PROSPERITY?

The privilege of a lifetime is being who you are.

~ Joseph Campbell, author

Prosperity is hard to define, but easy to see and feel when achieved. Being prosperous isn't necessarily about how much money you have, how many homes you own, or any of the other things people obsessed with material possessions covet.

Dictionary.com defines prosperity as, "a successful, flourishing, or thriving condition, especially in financial respects." Other definitions of prosperity include, "the condition of prospering; success or wealth."

The history of the word prosperity stems from the 12th century Old French word *prosprete*—derived from the Latin word *prosperitatem* which translates to "good fortune."

For increasing numbers of people, good fortune or being prosperous includes: living authentically; maintaining good health; and having fulfilling relationships, creative freedom, a sense of well-being, peace of mind, happiness and joy.

Prosperity, for some people, means achieving financial freedom. Prosperity also includes the ability to achieve your desires, whatever these may be, and being true to the vision you have for yourself and your life.

Coco Chanel once said, "There are people who have money and people who are rich. How many cares one loses when one decides not to be something, but to be someone."

When you commit to being the creator of your life and defining prosperity on your own terms, you choose to enrich your life and you become *"someone."* If earning a living from your writing is your goal, you choose to become a successful author.

MINING FOR GOLD

What does prosperity mean to you? Would a passive income that funds your lifestyle fit the bill? What about living and working anywhere in the world? Or do you need truckloads of sales on Amazon and buckets of savings in the bank to classify your life as "prosperous?"

How will you know when you have succeeded? Who are you, or who will you become?

What will the first line be in the story of your prosperous life?

2

WHAT DO YOU BELIEVE?

A large income is the best recipe for happiness I have heard of.

~ Jane Austen

"Research shows that 80 percent of individuals will never be financially free in the way they'd like to be, and 80 percent will never claim to be truly happy," writes T. Harv Eker in his book *Secrets of the Millionaire Mind: Mastering the Inner Game of Wealth*.

"The reason is simple," Eker writes, "Most people are unconscious. They are a little asleep at the wheel. They work and think on a superficial level of life—based only on what they can see. They live strictly in the visible world."

Yet, many of the things that influence your thoughts, feelings, and behaviors are invisible; a great many lurk in the realm of the subconscious mind.

The function of your subconscious mind is to store and retrieve data. Its job is to ensure that you respond exactly the way you are programmed.

"By the time you reach the age of 21, you've already permanently stored more than one hundred times the contents of the entire Encyclopedia Britannica," says motivational writer Brian Tracey.

And much of this information is rubbish, false, incomplete, or obsolete.

REPROGRAMMING Your Subconscious Beliefs

Your subconscious mind is like a huge memory bank. Its capacity is virtually unlimited. It permanently stores everything that ever happens to you. What is limited is your ability to consciously recall many of the scripts programmed into your mind.

You may not even be aware of limiting beliefs that are holding you back or placing a cap on your ability to earn a living from your writing.

One of the most important things you can commit to realizing is that you exist in more than the physical world. The mental world, the emotional world, and the spiritual world all exert a powerful influence over you—whether you are consciously tapping into them or not.

"What most people never realize is that the physical realm is merely a 'printout' of the other three," writes T. Harv Eker.

Any limiting and unhelpful beliefs or repressed experiences preventing you from becoming a prosperous author cannot be changed in the physical world. They can only be changed in the "program"—the mental, emotional, and spiritual worlds.

Which is why *The Prosperous Author: Developing a Millionaire Mindset* takes a holistic approach to success. Passion, joy, faith, prayer, dreams, purpose, and mindfulness practices are some of the strategies we'll discuss in this book.

You'll also learn how to develop a rock-solid belief in your ability to succeed. Building firm self-confidence will help you beat the naysayers and weather the inevitable setbacks with ease.

. . .

MINING FOR GOLD

How can you harness the power of the mental, emotional and spiritual worlds to reprogram your beliefs?

What evidence-based explanations do you have for the beliefs or rules you follow? How might the opposite also be true? How can you adjust your thinking?

3

YOUR MONEY BLUEPRINT

It's not enough to be in the right place at the right time. You have to be the right person in the right place at the right time.

~ T. Harv Eker

Your financial blueprint consists of a combination of your thoughts, feelings, and actions related to money.

It's formed primarily during childhood and the information or "programming" you received in the past. Imprinted upon you by parents, siblings, friends, authority figures, teachers, religious leaders, media, your culture, and other influential sources later in life, your beliefs, you sometimes find, are mistaken.

You may have heard, as I did growing up, that you'll never make a living from art. Or that art doesn't contribute anything of value to society.

The chances are high that you were actively discouraged and channeled into supposedly more "prosperous" or socially sanctioned pursuits, like being a lawyer or a doctor—or a good wife!

As Jeff Goins notes, for years, the fallacy of the starving artist has pervaded our culture, leaching into the minds of creative people and stifling their dreams.

But the evidence-based truth is that the world's most successful authors and artists do not starve. They thrive by leveraging off the power of their millionaire mindset and by capitalizing on their creative strengths.

Your thoughts and what you believe to be true for you influences your feelings, your energy, and ultimately your behavior.

What you believe, consciously or unconsciously, sets your income threshold.

Prosperous authors are never content with just scraping by. They believe they have the potential to create unlimited wealth—and they set out to achieve it.

So who are you? How do you think? What are your beliefs? What are your habits and traits? How do you really feel about money and your earning potential?

Answering these initial questions, and those below, will help your journey toward prosperity. You'll learn more strategies to help boost your self-awareness and co-create new liberating beliefs throughout this book.

Mining for Gold

What unhelpful beliefs were programmed into you as a child?

What messages have you heard, or do you continue to hear, about making a living from your art?

How are these messages influencing you?

Do you believe it's possible to make a substantial living from your writing? On a scale of 1-10, 10 being highest, what is the level of your self-belief?

EXCERPT: THE PROSPEROUS AUTHOR

DID YOU ENJOY THIS EXCERPT? **Available now from all good bookstores in paperback and eBook for immediate enjoyment.**

★★★★★ **If you want to make a living from your writing, read this book right now!**
By Amazon Customer on June 14, 2017
Format: Kindle Edition

It's one thing to write a book. It's another thing entirely to make a living at it. This book is a great primer for any writer with the dream of turning writing from a mere hobby into a career.

The wisdom and success stories she shares are invaluable to anyone who doesn't want to fall into the "starving artist" category that so many writers fear becoming. Of particular value is the info she shares on the importance of mindset - because without the right mindset, the would-be prosperous writer is likely to end up broke.

COPYRIGHT

Copyright © 2020 Cassandra Gaisford
Published by Blue Giraffe Publishing 2020

Blue Giraffe Publishing is a division of Worklife Solutions Ltd.

Cover Design by Cassandra Gaisford

All rights reserved. No part of this publication may be reproduced, distributed, or transmitted in any form or by any means, including photocopying, recording, or other electronic or mechanical methods, without the prior written permission of the author or publisher, except in the case of brief quotations embodied in reviews and certain other non-commercial uses permitted by copyright law.

    Neither the publisher nor the author are engaged in rendering professional advice or services to the individual reader. The ideas, procedures, and suggestions contained in this book are not intended as a substitute for psychotherapy, counseling, or consulting with your physician.

    The intent of the author is only to offer information of a general

COPYRIGHT

nature to help you in your quest for emotional, physical, and spiritual well-being.

Any use of information in this book is at the reader's discretion and risk. Neither the author nor the publisher can be held responsible for any loss, claim or damage arising out of the use, or misuse, of the suggestions made, the failure to take medical advice or for any material on third party websites.

ISBN PRINT: 978-0-9951072-4-3
   ISBN EBOOK: 978-0-9951072-3-6
     ISBN HARDCOVER:

First Edition

www.ingramcontent.com/pod-product-compliance
Lightning Source LLC
Chambersburg PA
CBHW030432010526
44118CB00011B/605